POEMS AND SATIRES

Poems

&

Satires

EDNA ST VINCENT MILLAY

edited by

TRISTRAM FANE SAUNDERS

CARCANET CLASSICS

First published in Great Britain in 2021 by
Carcanet
Alliance House, 30 Cross Street
Manchester M2 7AQ
www.carcanet.co.uk

A CIP catalogue record for this book is
available from the British Library.

ISBN 978 1 80017 167 1

Printed in Great Britain by SRP Ltd, Exeter, Devon

The publisher acknowledges financial
assistance from Arts Council England.

CONTENTS

LYRICS

SATIRES

POEMS AND SATIRES

'She was too beautiful to live among mortals,' Richard
Eberhart wrote of Edna St Vincent Millay, in his foreword
to the 1992 Carcanet edition of her poems. 'She symbolized
Platonic beauty.'

We hear a similar tone from an American art student who,
in 1922, spotted the famous 'Platonic beauty' in Paris—and
was appalled to learn she had an appetite. 'The girl sitting at
the next table was Edna St Vincent Millay,' this student wrote
in her diary. 'She was eating an enormous plate of sauerkraut
and sausages... Such a shock. I had always imagined her so
ethereal.'

The art student didn't exist. She was a creation of the
satirist Nancy Boyd, a name well known to readers of *Vanity
Fair*, where that diary-spoof appeared. But Boyd didn't exist
either—she was, in turn, a creation of Millay. Writing under
that guise, the poet published a series of short magazine
pieces, collected in book form as *Distressing Dialogues* in 1924
and out of print ever since.

These short satires are riotously funny, and innovative in their
range of forms. They move between fiction, drama, letters and
a kind of stand-up-comedy-cum-prose-poetry. One is a piece
of science fiction: an almanac from a *Handmaid's Tale*-esque
puritan future, where Prohibition has been extended to not only
alcohol but also tea and coffee. Though one or two references to
contemporary figures now require footnotes, Millay's portrait
of an American dystopia run by demagogues obsessed with the
'holy cause of Female Modesty' has lost none of its bite.

Throughout *Distressing Dialogues*, Millay rails against
pretension, conformity and society's double standards—with
the artifice of 'ethereal' femininity often in her crosshairs.
Time and again, she returns to two overlapping questions:

what it means to be a woman, and what it means to be an artist.

'The Implacable Aphrodite' takes the form of a short play script. The scene is 'a studied studio' where a self-satisfied male suitor visits a female sculptor. One stage direction reads: 'She is cruelly slicing a lemon, by means of a small dagger with which a Castilian nun has slain three matadors; it strikes him that she looks gentle and domestic.' At the risk of killing a good gag by dissection: Millay makes the closet drama form itself part of the joke. The reader sees the dagger as it really is; a theatre audience would share the suitor's ignorant male gaze.

As in those sketches, her experimental anti-war drama *Aria da Capo* (staged in 1919, published in 1921) sugars its anger with humour. Her harlequins may be calmly eating macaroons but there are dead bodies under the dining table. The best of Millay's handful of dramatic works, it is a remarkable forerunner to the Theatre of the Absurd, a Pirandellian meta-drama in which stock characters are aware of the roles in which they are trapped, one play interrupts another, and death holds the prompt-book.

Considering Millay's poetry in the context of these satires, we can hear her voice afresh. We can see her not as an idolised beauty, but as a proudly 'fierce and trivial' writer of flesh and acid, of sausage and sauerkraut. Millay's best work is sharp and self-aware, tightly controlled even when dramatising a loss of control, deeply engaged with poetic tradition yet bitingly contemporary.

One line of thought in Millay's poetry that her satires bring into sharper focus is the battle between body and mind, the 'treason/ Of my stout blood against my staggering brain'. It is a kind of Cartesian dualism: for this independent-minded poet, a human body is a strange and silly thing to have. Millay-as-Boyd writes: 'I am tired of feet. Feet are unpleasant. They are too flat. And there are too many toes on them.' In 'Menses', quite possibly the first poem explicitly about menstruation published in America, a version of the poet cries out: 'Heaven consign and damn/ To tedious Hell this body with its muddy feet in my mind!' A late poem calls the heart 'an idling engine, shaking the whole machine'; it is at once the seat of emotion and a mechanism of 'diastole and systole', unreliable in both roles.

As for sex? An enjoyable way to satisfy an appetite, but to any sensible individual no more shocking than a plate of sausages. Millay's unfinished satirical novel *Hardigut*, which she described as an allegory for attitudes to sex, imagined a world where 'people, otherwise perfectly sane and normal, do not eat in public, or discuss food except in innuendos and with ribald laughter.' In a Boyd piece, the Walrus from *Alice in Wonderland* suggests that instead of going on about sex—a tiresome cliché—to liven up conversation people could instead talk about indigestion. One sonnet questions the procreative urge through a pair of dispassionately rutting dinosaurs; another ends with the killer couplet, 'Whether or not we find what we are seeking/ Is idle, biologically speaking.'

And yet, sex has a way of getting tangled up with love. Without longing and heartbreak, and all their associated pains, great poems would never be written. One of Millay's finest sonnets compares her body of work to a tower built 'From what I had to build with; honest bone/ Is there, and anguish; pride; and burning thought;/ And lust is there, and nights not spent alone.'

It is this Millay, rather than the 'Platonic' ideal, that holds the public imagination. In 2018, the *Guardian* lamented that 'Millay's work has been overshadowed by her reputation' as 'a party girl poet' and 'a sexually adventurous bisexual', claiming that 'over the last half century' this image has 'eclipsed' the poetry. That account of Millay's reception is a little misleading, for three reasons.

First, popular interest in her reputation is not a development of the last half century. Millay's image overshadowed her work almost from the outset. In 1936 her first biographer, Elizabeth Atkins, presented Millay as 'the unrivalled embodiment of sex appeal, the It-girl of the hour, the Miss America of 1920'.

Second, Millay's image is not a blot on her work but an element of her work. It was a carefully constructed artistic achievement, developed through her writing and cemented in her charismatic public performances—honed through her experience as an actor and dramatist—on reading tours where she addressed audiences of thousands. 'Millay' was just as much an authorial creation as Nancy Boyd. Millay used the reader's assumed knowledge of her public image as a poetic device. One sonnet begins:

That love at length should find me out and bring
This fierce and trivial brow unto the dust,
Is, after all, I must confess, but just;
There is a subtle beauty in this thing,
A wry perfection

The Millay persona is key to the poem's central irony; that love should capture this particular poet, a poet who has so often shown herself to be too cool to fall in love, a poet who, after being felled by a force so patently beneath her, is still able to take a step back and observe the droll poetic justice of it.

Another wickedly ironic sonnet, 'I, being born a woman and distressed', illustrates the thesis of the critics Sandra M Gilbert and Susan Gubar. They consider both Millay and Marianne Moore as 'female female impersonators' who 'attired themselves in the artifice of the feminine so that they could produce ironic but vitally biographical portraits of the artist as that supreme fiction, woman.' It's a quality also apparent in her sardonic self-portrait 'E St V M', unpublished in her lifetime.

It is this that makes Millay as much a poet of the 2020s as the 1920s. The sonnets quoted above are of a piece with, say, the persona of Phoebe Stuckes's *Platinum Blonde*, or Hera Lindsay Bird's love poems, where glib irony is weaponised as 'a Trojan horse for sincerity'.

This particular Millay was, however, just one side to a persona that took on several aspects over the years—from the vatic, Romantic singer of early life-and-death poems such as 'Renascence' and 'The Blue-Flag in the Bog', to her final act as America's unofficial poet laureate in her campaigning work of the 1940s.

The third reason why it is wrong to complain that 'Millay's work has been overshadowed by her reputation' is that today her reputation casts no shadow. Most younger readers in 2021, encountering a few of her poems in anthologies, will naturally be unfamiliar with the narrative of her life. They will have no suspicion that she was once considered (as John Wilkinson put it in 2003) 'the most glamorous, sexually-dangerous and famous poet since Byron'.

Vincent—as Millay was called by friends and family—found success early and in an unusual way: she might be the only author to have risen to prominence by *losing* a competition. Born in 1892, she grew up in coastal Maine, living from 1904—the year of her parents' divorce—in a run-down neighbourhood of Camden beside the Megunticook River. When it burst its banks in winter, the poet and her two younger sisters would skate on the frozen floor of their flooded kitchen.

Her father left the family when she was young, and her mother was kept away for weeks at a time by her work as a nurse. As the oldest daughter, Millay was unwillingly thrust into the role of homemaker, a position from which she could see no escape. But in 1912, aged 20, she entered her poem 'Renascence' in a contest that offered cash awards for three winners, and a place in an anthology called *The Lyric Year* for a longlist of 100. It changed the course of her life.

'Renascence' didn't win, but it made the longlist. When *The Lyric Year* appeared, the poem's snubbing became a cause célèbre. The judges were widely criticised for choosing the wrong winners: *The New York Times* and *Chicago Evening Post* both called 'Renascence' the best thing in the book. A supernatural vision in tight tetrametric couplets, it prefigures a preoccupation with death that haunts all Millay's work—not as something to be feared in itself, but as a cruel negation of the vibrancy of life.

Incidentally, an early hint of Millay the satirist can be seen in a letter she sent the poet Arthur Davison Ficke, who had written to *The Lyric Year*'s editor about 'Renascence'. Ficke had called it 'a real vision, such as Coleridge might have seen,' adding: 'Are you at liberty to name the author? The little item about her in the back of the book is a marvel of humor. No sweet young thing of twenty ever ended a poem precisely where this one ends: it takes a brawny male of forty-five to do that.'

The letter was passed on to Millay, who replied: 'I simply will not be a "brawny male." Not that I have an aversion to brawny males; *au contraire, au contraire...* Is it that you consider brain and brawn so inseparable?—I have thought otherwise. Still, that is a matter of personal opinion. But, gentlemen: when a woman insists that she is twenty, you must not, must not call her forty-five. That is more than wicked; it is indiscreet.'

That summer, Millay recited 'Renascence' at a masquerade party held by the staff of a hotel where her sister Norma worked as a waitress. One guest within earshot was Caroline Dow, dean of the New York YWCA. Dazzled, Dow promised that very night to take up a collection among her wealthy friends, in order to send the poor prodigy to college.

She was true to her word. Millay was admitted to Vassar, despite flunking two of three entrance exams. There, the college president turned a blind eye to her constant misbehavior. He later recalled:

> [I] told her, 'I want you to know that you couldn't break any rule that would make me vote for your expulsion. I don't want to have any dead Shelleys on my doorstep and I don't care what you do.' She went to the window and looked out and she said, 'Well on those terms I think I can continue to live in this hellhole.'

When Millay nonetheless managed to get herself suspended—after sneaking out for a night at the opera—more than 100 of her classmates signed a petition calling (successfully) for her to be let off.

After graduating in 1917, she moved to Greenwich Village. Her first collection was published that year, and her poems were appearing widely in magazines. In March 1918 she wrote to the editor of *Poetry*:

> Dear Harriet Monroe,—
> Spring is here,—and I could be very happy, except that I am broke. Would you mind paying me *now* instead of on publication for those so stunning verses of mine which you have? I am become very, very thin, and have taken to smoking Virginia tobacco.
> Wistfully yours,
> Edna St Vincent Millay.
> PS I am *awfully* broke. Would you mind paying me a lot?

Monroe became one of her early champions, calling Millay 'perhaps the greatest woman poet since Sappho' in a 1924 essay noting 'how neatly she upsets the carefully built walls of convention which men have set up around their Ideal Woman'.

Monroe wrote of *Aria Da Capo*—staged in December 1919—that it was 'a masterpiece of irony sharp as Toledo steel'. But it was a fast-selling book of lighter verse, *A Few Figs from Thistles*, first published in 1920 by a Greenwich Village bookseller, which made her a household name—and a figurehead for a liberated, fast-living younger generation. To the Bohemians and flappers of 1920s New York, its opening poem was a manifesto:

My candle burns at both ends;
  It will not last the night;
But ah, my foes, and oh, my friends—
  It gives a lovely light!

In October 1920, she wrote: 'I am becoming famous [...] The current Vanity Fair has a whole page of my poems, and a photograph of me that looks about as much like me as it does like Arnold Bennett.' She was well known enough for the *New York Tribune* to run a contest asking for parodies ending with her name (eg: 'Laurel is green for a season, and love is sweet for a day;/ But love grows bitter with treason and Edna St Vincent Millay').

In 1923 she won the Pulitzer Prize for Poetry (the judges chose her work over that of Robert Frost and Wallace Stevens), and married a Dutch businessman, Eugen Boissevain. He was the widower of Inez Milholland, the famous feminist campaigner and war correspondent whom Millay had met at Vassar, and later elegised in a sonnet.

The extent of her early popularity and acclaim is difficult to exaggerate. Thomas Hardy was said to have remarked that America could boast only two great achievements: the skyscraper and the poetry of Edna St Vincent Millay.

On a reading tour in 1928, Millay met and fell in love with a 22-year-old poet called George Dillon. Their affair inspired her bestselling sonnet sequence *Fatal Interview*, and they later collaborated on a translation of Baudelaire's *Les Fleurs du Mal*.

Though her critical reputation waned in the 1930s, her 1939 collection *Huntsman, What Quarry?* contains some of her boldest and most incisive poetry—clear-eyed and unsentimental, and all the more moving for it. It also showed her willingness to experiment with flexible forms. 'Rendezvous', a rhymed poem of 14 lines describing an encounter with a younger man, is a kind of sagging sonnet. The elastic lines of its final quatrain test how long a rhyme can linger in the memory:

> Yet here I am, having told you of my quarrel with the taxi-driver
> over a line of Milton, and you laugh; and you are you, none
> other.
> Your laughter pelts my skin with small delicious blows.
> But I am perverse: I wish you had not scrubbed—with pumice, I
> suppose—
> The tobacco stains from your beautiful fingers. And I wish I did
> not feel like your mother.

After *Huntsman, What Quarry?*, Millay shifted the focus of her writing. Horrified by Nazi Germany, she became a propagandist, urging America to join the war and later supporting its wartime efforts. She was, by her own admission, writing 'not poems [but] posters'. *There Are No Islands Any More*, distributed as a broadside by the British War Relief society in 1939, is written in rhyming couplets beginning 'Dear isolationist, you are,/ So very, very insular!' It is far from her best work. Millay knew this. 'I have one thing to give in the service of my country—my reputation as a poet,' she wrote. 'If I can write just one poem that will turn the minds of a few to a more decent outlook […] what does it matter if I compose a bad line or lose my reputation as a craftsman?'

In 1942, when a poll suggested 30 per cent of Americans were willing to accept peace with Germany, her radio drama about the massacre of a Czech village, *The Murder of Lidice*, was broadcast to millions across the United States. What role her 1940s writing had in swaying the tide of national opinion cannot be estimated, but, as she predicted, she lost her reputation for craftsmanship. As the critic Merle Rubin put it, 'She seems to have caught more flak from the literary critics for supporting democracy than Ezra Pound did for championing fascism.' Millay exhausted herself working for the War Writers' Board and quit in 1943 following a nervous breakdown.

By the late 1940s Millay was drinking heavily and addicted to the morphine that she began taking in 1936, following a car-crash that left her with painful nerve damage in her spine for the rest of her life. The death of her husband in 1949 affected her deeply. On October 19 1950, she was found dead at their home in upstate New York, having fallen down a flight of stairs in the night.

Millay's reputation has fluctuated since her death. She was acknowledged as an influence by Anne Sexton and Sylvia Plath, but both were ambivalent about her work: it came to be seen as unfashionably sentimental, personal, un-modern. She was omitted entirely from the 1976 *Oxford Book of American Poetry*. But the work of feminist critics such as Gilbert and Gubar ushered in a re-evaluation around the time of her centenary, in which Carcanet's 1992 *Selected Poems*, edited by Colin Falck, played an important role.

It was through that pioneering edition that I fell in love with Millay's work. Falck, who passed away last year, celebrated Millay's 'existential fierceness', with a particular focus on those poems which showed her 'essential modernity', especially her late free verse. This was a necessary corrective to editions before and since which have erased Millay's later work entirely. For example, Penguin Random House's Modern Library *Selected*, marketed as 'a definitive collection', includes nothing later than *The Harp-Weaver, and Other Poems* (1923).

The title poem of that collection is one of Millay's least modern-seeming, but also one of her most popular. It has been taught in schools, recited on television and set to music by Johnny Cash. For one critic writing in the *Iowa Review* in 1992, the automatic answer to the question 'Who is Edna St Vincent Millay, anyway?' is 'She wrote "The Harp Weaver."' By omitting the poem, the previous Carcanet selection made a clear statement: this was not the Millay readers thought they knew.

In this new selection, I have tried to seek a middle path, striking a balance between including work which brought Millay acclaim in her lifetime, pieces which suggest her range as an artist, and those poems which best show the interplay between her roles as poet and satirist. I have also regularised a few small inconsistencies of punctuation and spelling, such as 'colour' for 'color'; Millay used both spellings interchangeably.

Millay's collection *Second April* was completed by 1919, though not published until 1921. For this reason, and to give a better sense of the development of her style, selections from *Second April* appear here before those from *A Few Figs from Thistles* (printed in various editions, with added poems, between 1920 and 1922).

One other aspect of the order of contents requires an explanation. It seems that Millay considered her sonnets to be a separate endeavour from her lyric poetry. In each of her individual collections, the sonnets are set apart, a choice underlined by the subtitle of *A Few Figs from Thistles*, 'Poems and Sonnets'. In her lifetime, they appeared in a volume of *Collected Sonnets*; in the posthumous *Collected Poems* edited by her sister Norma, they are given their own section. Following that precedent, the sonnets are also given their own section here. However, while each of Millay's individual volumes places the sonnets last, here they appear first.

I believe the sonnets are the best introduction to Millay's work, for the simple reason that they are her best work. When they use language that was already archaic in the poet's lifetime—'thou', 'thy'—it's often a signal to watch closely. In some poems, it could be taken as a way of giving potentially subversive ideas a cloak of respectability. At other times, it's a sincere engagement with the sonnet's already subversive tradition; the outrageous argument of 'Oh, think not I am faithful to a vow' is one any Elizabethan courtier would admire. Her narrative 'Sonnets from an Ungrafted Tree', meanwhile, is a masterpiece of psychological realism. The varied aspects of Millay's art come together in her sonnets. The love-poet, the elegist, the campaigner, the ironist and the virtuoso formalist all meet in one voice that declares: 'I will put chaos into fourteen lines'.

Select Bibliography

Millay, Edna St Vincent, *Collected Poems*, ed. Norma Millay (New York: HarperCollins, 2011; first published 1956).
——, *Three Plays* (London: Jonathan Cape, 1927).
——, *Conversation at Midnight* (New York and London: Harper & Brothers, 1937).
——, *Collected Sonnets of Edna St Vincent Millay* (New York and London: Harper & Brothers, 1941).
——, *The Murder of Lidice* (New York and London: Harper & Brothers, 1942).
——, *Letters of Edna St Vincent Millay*, ed. Allan Ross Macdougall (New York: Grosset & Dunlap, 1952).

——, *Selected Poems*, ed. Colin Falck (Manchester: Carcanet, 1992).

Boyd, Nancy, *Distressing Dialogues* (New York and London: Harper & Brothers, 1924).

Boyd, Nancy, 'Diary of an American Art Student in Paris', *Vanity Fair*, November 1922.

Dillon, George and Edna St Vincent Millay, *Flowers of Evil: From the French of Charles Baudelaire* (London: Hamish Hamilton, 1936).

Atkins, Elizabeth, *Edna St Vincent Millay and Her Times* (Chicago: The University of Chicago Press, 1936).

Epstein, Daniel Mark, *What Lips My Lips Have Kissed: The Loves and Love Poems of Edna St Vincent Millay* (New York: Henry Holt and Company, 2001).

Gilbert, Sandra M and Susan Gubar, 'Female Female Impersonators: The Fictive Music of Edna St Vincent Millay and Marianne Moore', in *No Man's Land: The Place of the Woman Writer in the Twentieth Century: Volume 3, Letters from the Front* (New Haven and London: Yale University Press, 1994).

Martin, W, 'Review:… And Now to Introduce: Edna St. Vincent Millay!', *The Iowa Review* Vol 22 No 3 (Fall, 1992).

Milford, Nancy, *Savage Beauty: The Life of Edna St Vincent Millay* (New York: Random House, 2001).

Monroe, Harriet, 'Edna St Vincent Millay', *Poetry* Vol 24 No 5, August 1924.

Ong, Amandas, 'Edna St Vincent Millay's poetry has been eclipsed by her personal life—let's change that', *The Guardian,* February 22 2018.

Rubin, Merle, 'Lyrical, Rebellious and Almost Forgotten', *The Wall Street Journal*, September 6 2001.

Wilkinson, John, 'Chamber Attitudes,' *Jacket* 21, February 2003.

Acknowledgements

The editor thanks Kilmeny Denny, Andrew Latimer, Ali Lewis, Lucia Morello, Cal Revely-Calder and Michael Schmidt for their support in preparing this book for publication.

SONNETS

If I should learn, in some quite casual way,
That you were gone, not to return again—
Read from the back-page of a paper, say,
Held by a neighbour in a subway train,
How at the corner of this avenue
And such a street (so are the papers filled)
A hurrying man—who happened to be you—
At noon today had happened to be killed,
I should not cry aloud—I could not cry
Aloud, or wring my hands in such a place—
I should but watch the station lights rush by
With a more careful interest on my face,
Or raise my eyes and read with greater care
Where to store furs and how to treat the hair.

BLUEBEARD

This door you might not open, and you did;
So enter now, and see for what slight thing
You are betrayed... Here is no treasure hid,
No cauldron, no clear crystal mirroring
The sought-for Truth, no heads of women slain
For greed like yours, no writhings of distress;
But only what you see... Look yet again;
An empty room, cobwebbed and comfortless.
Yet this alone out of my life I kept
Unto myself, lest any know me quite;
And you did so profane me when you crept
Unto the threshold of this room tonight
That I must never more behold your face.
This now is yours. I seek another place.

Time does not bring relief; you all have lied
Who told me time would ease me of my pain!
I miss him in the weeping of the rain;
I want him at the shrinking of the tide;
The old snows melt from every mountain-side,
And last year's leaves are smoke in every lane;
But last year's bitter loving must remain
Heaped on my heart, and my old thoughts abide.
There are a hundred places where I fear
To go,—so with his memory they brim.
And entering with relief some quiet place
Where never fell his foot or shone his face
I say, 'There is no memory of him here!'
And so stand stricken, so remembering him.

Only until this cigarette is ended,
A little moment at the end of all,
While on the floor the quiet ashes fall,
And in the firelight to a lance extended,
Bizarrely with the jazzing music blended,
The broken shadow dances on the wall,
I will permit my memory to recall
The vision of you, by all my dreams attended.
And then adieu,—farewell!—the dream is done.
Yours is a face of which I can forget
The colour and the features, every one,
The words not ever, and the smiles not yet;
But in your day this moment is the sun
Upon a hill, after the sun has set.

I shall forget you presently, my dear,
So make the most of this, your little day,
Your little month, your little half a year,
Ere I forget, or die, or move away,
And we are done forever; by and by
I shall forget you, as I said, but now,
If you entreat me with your loveliest lie
I will protest you with my favourite vow.
I would indeed that love were longer-lived,
And oaths were not so brittle as they are,
But so it is, and nature has contrived
To struggle on without a break thus far,—
Whether or not we find what we are seeking
Is idle, biologically speaking.

Oh, think not I am faithful to a vow!
Faithless am I save to love's self alone.
Were you not lovely I would leave you now:
After the feet of beauty fly my own.
Were you not still my hunger's rarest food,
And water ever to my wildest thirst,
I would desert you—think not but I would!—
And seek another as I sought you first.
But you are mobile as the veering air,
And all your charms more changeful than the tide,
Wherefore to be inconstant is no care:
I have but to continue at your side.
So wanton, light and false, my love, are you,
I am most faithless when I am most true.

What lips my lips have kissed, and where, and why,
I have forgotten, and what arms have lain
Under my head till morning; but the rain
Is full of ghosts tonight, that tap and sigh
Upon the glass and listen for reply,
And in my heart there stirs a quiet pain
For unremembered lads that not again
Will turn to me at midnight with a cry.
Thus in the winter stands the lonely tree,
Nor knows what birds have vanished one by one,
Yet knows its boughs more silent than before:
I cannot say what loves have come and gone,
I only know that summer sang in me
A little while, that in me sings no more.

That Love at length should find me out and bring
This fierce and trivial brow unto the dust,
Is, after all, I must confess, but just;
There is a subtle beauty in this thing,
A wry perfection; wherefore now let sing
All voices how into my throat is thrust,
Unwelcome as Death's own, Love's bitter crust,
All criers proclaim it, and all steeples ring.
This being done, there let the matter rest.
What more remains is neither here nor there.
That you requite me not is plain to see.
Myself your slave herein have I confessed:
Thus far, indeed, the world may mock at me;
But if I suffer, it is my own affair.

I, being born a woman and distressed
By all the needs and notions of my kind,
Am urged by your propinquity to find
Your person fair, and feel a certain zest
To bear your body's weight upon my breast:
So subtly is the fume of life designed,
To clarify the pulse and cloud the mind,
And leave me once again undone, possessed.
Think not for this, however, the poor treason
Of my stout blood against my staggering brain,
I shall remember you with love, or season
My scorn with pity,—let me make it plain:
I find this frenzy insufficient reason
For conversation when we meet again.

I shall go back again to the bleak shore
And build a little shanty on the sand,
In such a way that the extremest band
Of brittle seaweed will escape my door
But by a yard or two; and nevermore
Shall I return to take you by the hand;
I shall be gone to what I understand,
And happier than I ever was before.
The love that stood a moment in your eyes,
The words that lay a moment on your tongue,
Are one with all that in a moment dies,
A little under-said and over-sung.
But I shall find the sullen rocks and skies
Unchanged from what they were when I was young.

Euclid alone has looked on Beauty bare.
Let all who prate of Beauty hold their peace,
And lay them prone upon the earth and cease
To ponder on themselves, the while they stare
At nothing, intricately drawn nowhere
In shapes of shifting lineage; let geese
Gabble and hiss, but heroes seek release
From dusty bondage into luminous air.
O blinding hour, O holy, terrible day,
When first the shaft into his vision shone
Of light anatomized! Euclid alone
Has looked on beauty bare. Fortunate they
Who, though once only and then but far away,
Have heard her massive sandal set on stone.

SONNETS FROM AN UNGRAFTED TREE

I

So she came back into his house again
And watched beside his head until he died,
Loving him not at all. The winter rain
Splashed in the painted butter-tub outside,
Where once her red geraniums had stood,
Where still their rotted stalks were to be seen;
The thin log snapped; and she went out for wood,
Bareheaded, running the few steps between
The house and shed; there, from the sodden eaves
Blown back and forth on ragged ends of twine,
Saw the dejected creeping jinny-vine,
(And one, big-aproned, blithe, with stiff blue sleeves
Rolled to the shoulder that warm day in spring,
Who planted seeds, musing ahead to their far blossoming).

II

The last white sawdust on the floor was grown
Gray as the first, so long had he been ill;
The axe was nodding in the block; fresh-blown
And foreign came the rain across the sill,
But on the roof so steadily it drummed
She could not think a time it might not be—
In hazy summer, when the hot air hummed
With mowing, and locusts rising raspingly,
When that small bird with iridescent wings
And long incredible sudden silver tongue
Had just flashed (and yet maybe not!) among
The dwarf nasturtiums—when no sagging springs
Of shower were in the whole bright sky, somehow
Upon this roof the rain would drum as it was drumming now.

III

She filled her arms with wood, and set her chin
Forward, to hold the highest stick in place,
No less afraid than she had always been
Of spiders up her arms and on her face,
But too impatient for a careful search
Or a less heavy loading, from the heap
Selecting hastily small sticks of birch,
For their curled bark, that instantly will leap
Into a blaze, nor thinking to return
Some day, distracted, as of old, to find
Smooth, heavy, round, green logs with a wet, gray rind
Only, and knotty chunks that will not burn,
(That day when dust is on the wood-box floor,
And some old catalogue, and a brown, shriveled apple core).

IV

The white bark writhed and sputtered like a fish
Upon the coals, exuding odorous smoke.
She knelt and blew, in a surging desolate wish
For comfort; and the sleeping ashes woke
And scattered to the hearth, but no thin fire
Broke suddenly, the wood was wet with rain.
Then, softly stepping forth from her desire,
(Being mindful of like passion hurled in vain
Upon a similar task, in other days)
She thrust her breath against the stubborn coal,
Bringing to bear upon its hilt the whole
Of her still body... there sprang a little blaze...
A pack of hounds, the flame swept up the flue!—
And the blue night stood flattened against the window, staring through.

V

A wagon stopped before the house; she heard
The heavy oilskins of the grocer's man
Slapping against his legs. Of a sudden whirred
He heart like a frightened partridge, and she ran
And slid the bolt, leaving his entrance free;
Then in the cellar way till he was gone
Hid, breathless, praying that he might not see
The chair sway she had laid her hand upon
In passing. Sour and damp from that dark vault
Arose to her the well-remembered chill;
She saw the narrow wooden stairway still
Plunging into the earth, and the thin salt
Crusting the crocks; until she knew him far,
So stood, with listening eyes upon the empty doughnut jar.

VI

Then cautiously she pushed the cellar door
And stepped into the kitchen—saw the track
Of muddy weather boots across the floor,
The many paper parcels in a stack
Upon the dresser; with accustomed care
Removed the twine and put the wrappings by,
Folded, and the bags flat, that with an air
Of ease had been whipped open skillfully,
To the gape of children. Treacherously dear
And simple was the dull, familiar task.
And so it was she came at length to ask:
How came the soda there? The sugar here?
Then the dream broke. Silent, she brought the mop,
And forced the trade-slip on the nail that held his razor strop.

VII

One way there was of muting in the mind
A little while the ever-clamorous care;
And there was rapture, of a decent kind,
In making mean and ugly objects fair:
Soft-sooted kettle-bottoms, that had been
Time after time set in above the fire,
Faucets, and candlesticks, corroded green,
To mine again from quarry; to attire
The shelves in paper petticoats, and tack
New oilcloth in the ringed-and-rotten's place,
Polish the stove till you could see your face,
And after nightfall rear an aching back
In a changed kitchen, bright as a new pin,
An advertisement, far too fine to cook a supper in.

VIII

She let them leave their jellies at the door
And go away, reluctant, down the walk.
She heard them talking as they passed before
The blind, but could not quite make out their talk
For noise in the room—the sudden heavy fall
And roll of a charred log, and the roused shower
Of snapping sparks; then sharply from the wall
The unforgivable crowing of the hour.
One instant set ajar, her quiet ear
Was stormed and forced by the full rout of day:
The rasp of a saw, the fussy cluck and bray
Of hens, the wheeze of a pump, she needs must hear;
She inescapably must endure to feel
Across her teeth the grinding of a backing wagon wheel.

IX

Not over-kind nor over-quick in study
Nor skilled in sports nor beautiful was he,
Who had come into her life when anybody
Would have been welcome, so in need was she.
They had become acquainted in this way:
He flashed a mirror in her eyes at school;
By which he was distinguished. From that day
They went about together, as a rule.
She told, in secret and with whispering,
How he had flashed a mirror in her eyes;
And as she told, it struck her with surprise
That this was not so wonderful a thing.
But what's the odds?—It's pretty nice to know
You've got a friend to keep you company everywhere you go.

X

She had forgotten how the August night
Was level as a lake beneath the moon,
In which she swam a little, losing sight
Of shore; and how the boy, who was at noon
Simple enough, not different from the rest,
Wore now a pleasant mystery as he went,
Which seemed to her an honest enough test
Whether she loved him, and she was content.
So loud, so loud the million crickets' choir...
So sweet the night, so long-drawn-out and late...
And if the man were not her spirit's mate,
Why was her body sluggish with desire?
Stark on the open field the moonlight fell,
But the oak tree's shadow was deep and black and secret as a well.

XI

It came into her mind, seeing how the snow
Was gone, and the brown grass exposed again,
And clothes-pins, and an apron—long ago,
In some white storm that sifted through the pane
And sent her forth reluctantly at last
To gather in, before the line gave way,
Garments, board-stiff, that galloped on the blast
Clashing like angel armies in a fray,
An apron long ago in such a night
Blown down and buried in the deepening drift,
To lie till April thawed it back to sight,
Forgotten, quaint and novel as a gift—
It struck her, as she pulled and pried and tore,
That here was spring, and the whole year to be lived through
    once more.

XII

Tenderly, in those times, as though she fed
An ailing child—with sturdy propping up
Of its small, feverish body in the bed,
And steadying of its hands about the cup—
She gave her husband of her body's strength,
Thinking of men, what helpless things they were,
Until he turned and fell asleep at length,
And stealthily stirred the night and spoke to her.
Familiar, at such moments, like a friend,
Whistled far off the long, mysterious train,
And she could see in her mind's vision plain
The magic World, where cities stood on end...
Remote from where she lay—and yet—between,
Save for something asleep beside her, only the window screen.

XIII

From the wan dream that was her waking day,
Wherein she journeyed, borne along the ground
Without her own volition in some way,
Or fleeing, motionless, with feet fast bound,
Or running silent through a silent house
Sharply remembered from an earlier dream,
Upstairs, down other stairs, fearful to rouse,
Regarding him, the wide and empty scream
Of a strange sleeper on a malignant bed,
And all the time not certain if it were
Herself so doing or some one like to her,
From this wan dream that was her daily bread,
Sometimes, at night, incredulous, she would wake—
A child, blowing bubbles that the chairs and carpet did not break!

XIV

She had a horror he would die at night.
And sometimes when the light began to fade
She could not keep from noticing how white
The birches looked—and then she would be afraid,
Even with a lamp, to go about the house
And lock the windows; and as night wore on
Toward morning, if a dog howled, or a mouse
Squeaked in the floor, long after it was gone
Her flesh would sit awry on her. By day
She would forget somewhat, and it would seem
A silly thing to go with just this dream
And get a neighbour to come at night and stay.
But it would strike her sometimes, making the tea:
She had kept that kettle boiling all night long, for company.

XV

There was upon the sill a pencil mark,
Vital with shadow when the sun stood still
At noon, but now, because the day was dark,
It was a pencil mark upon the sill.
And the mute clock, maintaining ever the same
Dead moment, blank and vacant of itself,
Was a pink shepherdess, a picture frame,
A shell marked Souvenir, there on the shelf.
Whence it occurred to her that he might be,
The mainspring being broken in his mind,
A clock himself, if one were so inclined,
That stood at twenty minutes after three—
The reason being for this, it might be said,
That things in death were neither clocks nor people, but only dead.

XVI

The doctor asked her what she wanted done
With him, that could not lie there many days.
And she was shocked to see how life goes on
Even after death, in irritating ways;
And mused how if he had not died at all
'Twould have been easier—then there need not be
The stiff disorder of a funeral
Everywhere, and the hideous industry,
And crowds of people calling her by name
And questioning her, she'd never seen before,
But only watching by his bed once more
And sitting silent if a knocking came…
She said at length, feeling the doctor's eyes,
'I don't know what you do exactly when a person dies.'

XVII

Gazing upon him now, severe and dead,
It seemed a curious thing that she had lain
Beside him many a night in that cold bed,
And that had been which would not be again.
From his desirous body the great heat
Was gone at last, it seemed, and the taut nerves
Loosened forever. Formally the sheet
Set forth for her today those heavy curves
And lengths familiar as the bedroom door.
She was as one who enters, sly, and proud,
To where her husband speaks before a crowd,
And sees a man she never saw before—
The man who eats his victuals at her side,
Small, and absurd, and hers: for once, not hers, unclassified.

SONNET TO GATH

Country of hunchbacks!—where the strong, straight spine,
Jeered at by crooked children, makes his way
Through by-streets at the kindest hour of day,
Till he deplore his stature, and incline
To measure manhood with a gibbous line;
Till out of loneliness, being flawed with clay,
He stoop into his neighbour's house and say,
'Your roof is low for me—the fault is mine.'
Dust in an urn long since, dispersed and dead
Is great Apollo; and the happier he;
Since who amongst you all would lift a head
At a god's radiance on the mean door-tree,
Saving to run and hide your dates and bread,
And cluck your children in about your knee?

TO INEZ MILHOLLAND

*Read in Washington, November eighteenth, 1923, at the unveiling of
a statue of three leaders in the cause of Equal Rights for Women*

Upon this marble bust that is not I
Lay the round, formal wreath that is not fame;
But in the forum of my silenced cry
Root ye the living tree whose sap is flame.
I, that was proud and valiant, am no more;—
Save as a dream that wanders wide and late,
Save as a wind that rattles the stout door,
Troubling the ashes in the sheltered grate.
The stone will perish; I shall be twice dust.
Only my standard on a taken hill
Can cheat the mildew and the red-brown rust
And make immortal my adventurous will.
Even now the silk is tugging at the staff:
Take up the song; forget the epitaph.

from FATAL INTERVIEW

XI

Not in a silver casket cool with pearls
Or rich with red corundum or with blue,
Locked, and the key withheld, as other girls
Have given their loves, I give my love to you;
Not in a lovers'-knot, not in a ring
Worked in such fashion, and the legend plain—
Semper fidelis, where a secret spring
Kennels a drop of mischief for the brain;
Love in the open hand, no thing but that,
Ungemmed, unhidden, wishing not to hurt,
As one should bring you cowslips in a hat
Swung from the hand, or apples in her skirt,
I bring you, calling out as children do:
'Look what I have—And these are all for you.'

XXX

Love is not all: it is not meat nor drink
Nor slumber nor a roof against the rain;
Nor yet a floating spar to men that sink
And rise and sink and rise and sink again;
Love can not fill the thickened lung with breath,
Nor clean the blood, nor set the fractured bone;
Yet many a man is making friends with death
Even as I speak, for lack of love alone.
It well may be that in a difficult hour,
Pinned down by pain and moaning for release,
Or nagged by want past resolution's power,
I might be driven to sell your love for peace,
Or trade the memory of this night for food.
It well may be. I do not think I would.

XXXIII

Sorrowful dreams remembered after waking
Shadow with dolour all the candid day;
Even as I read, the silly tears out-breaking
Splash on my hands and shut the page away...
Grief at the root, a dark and secret dolour,
Harder to bear than wind-and-weather grief,
Clutching the rose, draining its cheek of colour,
Drying the bud, curling the opened leaf.
Deep is the pond—although the edge be shallow,
Frank in the sun, revealing fish and stone,
Climbing ashore to turtle-head and mallow—
Black at the centre beats a heart unknown.
Desolate dreams pursue me out of sleep;
Weeping I wake; waking, I weep, I weep.

XLI

I said in the beginning, did I not?—
Prophetic of the end, though unaware
How light you took me, ignorant that you thought
I spoke to see my breath upon the air;
If you walk east at daybreak from the town
To the cliff's foot, by climbing steadily
You cling at noon whence there is no way down
But to go toppling backward to the sea.
And not for birds nor birds'-eggs, so they say,
But for a flower that in these fissures grows,
Forms have been seen to move throughout the day
Skyward; but what its name is no one knows.
'Tis said you find beside them on the sand
This flower, relinquished by the broken hand.

from EPITAPH FOR THE RACE OF MAN

II

When Death was young and bleaching bones were few,
A moving hill against the risen day
The dinosaur at morning made his way,
And dropped his dung upon the blazing dew;
Trees with no name that now are agate grew
Lushly beside him in the steamy clay;
He woke and hungered, rose and stalked his prey,
And slept contented, in a world he knew.
In punctual season, with the race in mind,
His consort held aside her heavy tail,
And took the seed; and heard the seed confined
Roar in her womb; and made a nest to hold
A hatched-out conqueror... but to no avail:
The veined and fertile eggs are long since cold.

III

Cretaceous bird, your giant claw no lime
From bark of holly bruised or mistletoe
Could have arrested, could have held you so
Through fifty million years of jostling time;
Yet cradled with you in the catholic slime
Of the young ocean's tepid lapse and flow
Slumbered an agent, weak in embryo,
Should grip you straitly, in its sinewy prime.
What bright collision in the zodiac brews,
What mischief dimples at the planet's core
For shark, for python, for the dove that coos
Under the leaves?—what frosty fate's in store
For the warm blood of man,—man, out of ooze
But lately crawled, and climbing up the shore?

IV

O Earth, unhappy planet born to die,
Might I your scribe and your confessor be,
What wonders must you not relate to me
Of Man, who when his destiny was high
Strode like the sun into the middle sky
And shone an hour, and who so bright as he,
And like the sun went down into the sea,
Leaving no spark to be remembered by.
But no; you have not learned in all these years
To tell the leopard and the newt apart;
Man, with his singular laughter, his droll tears,
His engines and his conscience and his art,
Made but a simple sound upon your ears:
The patient beating of the animal heart.

V

When Man is gone and only gods remain
To stride the world, their mighty bodies hung
With golden shields, and golden curls outflung
Above their childish foreheads; when the plain
Round skull of Man is lifted and again
Abandoned by the ebbing wave, among
The sand and pebbles of the beach,—what tongue
Will tell the marvel of the human brain?
Heavy with music once this windy shell,
Heavy with knowledge of the clustered stars;
The one-time tenant of this draughty hall
Himself, in learned pamphlet, did foretell,
After some aeons of study jarred by wars,
This toothy gourd, this head emptied of all.

I too beneath your moon, almighty Sex,
Go forth at nightfall crying like a cat,
Leaving the lofty tower I laboured at
For birds to foul and boys and girls to vex
With tittering chalk; and you, and the long necks
Of neighbours sitting where their mothers sat
Are well aware of shadowy this and that
In me, that's neither noble nor complex.
Such as I am, however, I have brought
To what it is, this tower; it is my own;
Though it was reared To Beauty, it was wrought
From what I had to build with; honest bone
Is there, and anguish; pride; and burning thought;
And lust is there, and nights not spent alone.

I will put Chaos into fourteen lines
And keep him there; and let him thence escape
If he be lucky; let him twist, and ape
Flood, fire, and demon—his adroit designs
Will strain to nothing in the strict confines
Of this sweet Order, where, in pious rape,
I hold his essence and amorphous shape,
Till he with Order mingles and combines.
Past are the hours, the years, of our duress,
His arrogance, our awful servitude:
I have him. He is nothing more nor less
Than something simple not yet understood;
I shall not even force him to confess;
Or answer. I will only make him good.

LYRICS

RENASCENCE

All I could see from where I stood
Was three long mountains and a wood;
I turned and looked another way,
And saw three islands in a bay.
So with my eyes I traced the line
Of the horizon, thin and fine,
Straight around till I was come
Back to where I'd started from;
And all I saw from where I stood
Was three long mountains and a wood.

Over these things I could not see;
These were the things that bounded me;
And I could touch them with my hand,
Almost, I thought, from where I stand.
And all at once things seemed so small
My breath came short, and scarce at all.

But, sure, the sky is big, I said;
Miles and miles above my head;
So here upon my back I'll lie
And look my fill into the sky.
And so I looked, and, after all,
The sky was not so very tall.
The sky, I said, must somewhere stop,
And—sure enough!—I see the top!
The sky, I thought, is not so grand;
I 'most could touch it with my hand!
And reaching up my hand to try,
I screamed to feel it touch the sky.

I screamed, and—lo!—Infinity
Came down and settled over me;
Forced back my scream into my chest,
Bent back my arm upon my breast,
And, pressing of the Undefined
The definition on my mind,
Held up before my eyes a glass
Through which my shrinking sight did pass
Until it seemed I must behold
Immensity made manifold;
Whispered to me a word whose sound
Deafened the air for worlds around,
And brought unmuffled to my ears
The gossiping of friendly spheres,
The creaking of the tented sky,
The ticking of Eternity.

I saw and heard, and knew at last
The How and Why of all things, past,
And present, and forevermore.
The Universe, cleft to the core,
Lay open to my probing sense
That, sick'ning, I would fain pluck thence
But could not,—nay! But needs must suck
At the great wound, and could not pluck
My lips away till I had drawn
All venom out.—Ah, fearful pawn!
For my omniscience paid I toll
In infinite remorse of soul.

All sin was of my sinning, all
Atoning mine, and mine the gall
Of all regret. Mine was the weight
Of every brooded wrong, the hate

That stood behind each envious thrust,
Mine every greed, mine every lust.

And all the while for every grief,
Each suffering, I craved relief
With individual desire,—
Craved all in vain! And felt fierce fire
About a thousand people crawl;
Perished with each,—then mourned for all!

A man was starving in Capri;
He moved his eyes and looked at me;
I felt his gaze, I heard his moan,
And knew his hunger as my own.
I saw at sea a great fog bank
Between two ships that struck and sank;
A thousand screams the heavens smote;
And every scream tore through my throat.

No hurt I did not feel, no death
That was not mine; mine each last breath
That, crying, met an answering cry
From the compassion that was I.
All suffering mine, and mine its rod;
Mine, pity like the pity of God.

Ah, awful weight! Infinity
Pressed down upon the finite Me!
My anguished spirit, like a bird,
Beating against my lips I heard;
Yet lay the weight so close about
There was no room for it without.
And so beneath the weight lay I
And suffered death, but could not die.

Long had I lain thus, craving death,
When quietly the earth beneath
Gave way, and inch by inch, so great
At last had grown the crushing weight,
Into the earth I sank till I
Full six feet under ground did lie,
And sank no more,—there is no weight
Can follow here, however great.
From off my breast I felt it roll,
And as it went my tortured soul
Burst forth and fled in such a gust
That all about me swirled the dust.

Deep in the earth I rested now;
Cool is its hand upon the brow
And soft its breast beneath the head
Of one who is so gladly dead.
And all at once, and over all
The pitying rain began to fall;
I lay and heard each pattering hoof
Upon my lowly, thatched roof,
And seemed to love the sound far more
Than ever I had done before.
For rain it hath a friendly sound
To one who's six feet underground;
And scarce the friendly voice or face:
A grave is such a quiet place.

The rain, I said, is kind to come
And speak to me in my new home.
I would I were alive again
To kiss the fingers of the rain,
To drink into my eyes the shine
Of every slanting silver line,

To catch the freshened, fragrant breeze
From drenched and dripping apple-trees.
For soon the shower will be done,
And then the broad face of the sun
Will laugh above the rain-soaked earth
Until the world with answering mirth
Shakes joyously, and each round drop
Rolls, twinkling, from its grass-blade top.

How can I bear it; buried here,
While overhead the sky grows clear
And blue again after the storm?
O, multi-coloured, multiform,
Beloved beauty over me,
That I shall never, never see
Again! Spring-silver, autumn-gold,
That I shall never more behold!
Sleeping your myriad magics through,
Close-sepulchred away from you!
O God, I cried, give me new birth,
And put me back upon the earth!
Upset each cloud's gigantic gourd
And let the heavy rain, down-poured
In one big torrent, set me free,
Washing my grave away from me!

I ceased; and through the breathless hush
That answered me, the far-off rush
Of herald wings came whispering
Like music down the vibrant string
Of my ascending prayer, and—crash!
Before the wild wind's whistling lash
The startled storm-clouds reared on high
And plunged in terror down the sky,

And the big rain in one black wave
Fell from the sky and struck my grave.

I know not how such things can be;
I only know there came to me
A fragrance such as never clings
To aught save happy living things;
A sound as of some joyous elf
Singing sweet songs to please himself,
And, through and over everything,
A sense of glad awakening.
The grass, a-tiptoe at my ear,
Whispering to me I could hear;
I felt the rain's cool finger-tips
Brushed tenderly across my lips,
Laid gently on my sealed sight,
And all at once the heavy night
Fell from my eyes and I could see,—
A drenched and dripping apple-tree,
A last long line of silver rain,
A sky grown clear and blue again.
And as I looked a quickening gust
Of wind blew up to me and thrust
Into my face a miracle
Of orchard-breath, and with the smell,—
I know not how such things can be!—
I breathed my soul back into me.

Ah! Up then from the ground sprang I
And hailed the earth with such a cry
As is not heard save from a man
Who has been dead, and lives again.
About the trees my arms I wound;

Like one gone mad I hugged the ground;
I raised my quivering arms on high;
I laughed and laughed into the sky,
Till at my throat a strangling sob
Caught fiercely, and a great heart-throb
Sent instant tears into my eyes;
O God, I cried, no dark disguise
Can e'er hereafter hide from me
Thy radiant identity!

Thou canst not move across the grass
But my quick eyes will see Thee pass,
Nor speak, however silently,
But my hushed voice will answer Thee.
I know the path that tells Thy way
Through the cool eve of every day;
God, I can push the grass apart
And lay my finger on Thy heart!

The world stands out on either side
No wider than the heart is wide;
Above the world is stretched the sky,—
No higher than the soul is high.
The heart can push the sea and land
Farther away on either hand;
The soul can split the sky in two,
And let the face of God shine through.
But East and West will pinch the heart
That can not keep them pushed apart;
And he whose soul is flat—the sky
Will cave in on him by and by.

God had called us, and we came;
   Our loved Earth to ashes left;
Heaven was a neighbour's house,
   Open flung to us, bereft.

Gay the lights of Heaven showed,
   And 'twas God who walked ahead;
Yet I wept along the road,
   Wanting my own house instead.

Wept unseen, unheeded cried,
   'All you things my eyes have kissed,
Fare you well! We meet no more,
   Lovely, lovely tattered mist!

Weary wings that rise and fall
   All day long above the fire!'
(Red with heat was every wall,
   Rough with heat was every wire)

'Fare you well, you little winds
   That the flying embers chase!
Fare you well, you shuddering day,
   With your hands before your face!

And, ah, blackened by strange blight,
   Or to a false sun unfurled,
Now forevermore goodbye,
   All the gardens in the world!

On the windless hills of Heaven,
    That I have no wish to see,
White, eternal lilies stand,
    By a lake of ebony.

But the Earth forevermore
    Is a place where nothing grows,—
Dawn will come, and no bud break;
    Evening, and no blossom close.

Spring will come, and wander slow
    Over an indifferent land,
Stand beside an empty creek,
    Hold a dead seed in her hand.'

—

God had called us, and we came,
    But the blessèd road I trod
Was a bitter road to me,
    And at heart I questioned God.

'Though in Heaven,' I said, 'be all
    That the heart would most desire,
Held Earth naught save souls of sinners
    Worth the saving from a fire?

Withered grass,—the wasted growing!
    Aimless ache of laden boughs!'
Little things God had forgotten
    Called me, from my burning house.

'Though in Heaven,' I said, 'be all
    That the eye could ask to see,
All the things I ever knew
    Are this blaze in back of me.'

'Though in Heaven,' I said, 'be all
    That the ear could think to lack,
All the things I ever knew
    Are this roaring at my back.'

———

It was God who walked ahead,
    Like a shepherd to the fold;
In his footsteps fared the weak,
    And the weary and the old,

Glad enough of gladness over,
    Ready for the peace to be,—
But a thing God had forgotten
    Was the growing bones of me.

And I drew a bit apart,
    And I lagged a bit behind,
And I thought on Peace Eternal,
    Lest He look into my mind;

And I gazed upon the sky,
    And I thought of Heavenly Rest,—
And I slipped away like water
    Through the fingers of the blest!

All their eyes were fixed on Glory,
    Not a glance brushed over me;
'Alleluia! Alleluia!'
    Up the road,—and I was free.
And my heart rose like a freshet,
    And it swept me on before,
Giddy as a whirling stick,
    Till I felt the earth once more.

—

All the Earth was charred and black,
    Fire had swept from pole to pole;
And the bottom of the sea
    Was as brittle as a bowl;

And the timbered mountain-top
    Was as naked as a skull,—
Nothing left, nothing left,
    Of the Earth so beautiful!

'Earth,' I said, 'how can I leave you?'
    'You are all I have,' I said;
'What is left to take my mind up,
    Living always, and you dead?'

'Speak!' I said, 'Oh, tell me something!
    Make a sign that I can see!
For a keepsake! To keep always!
    Quick!—before God misses me!'

And I listened for a voice;—
    But my heart was all I heard;
Not a screech-owl, not a loon,
    Not a tree-toad said a word.

And I waited for a sign;—
   Coals and cinders, nothing more;
And a little cloud of smoke
   Floating on a valley floor.

And I peered into the smoke
   Till it rotted, like a fog:—
There, encompassed round by fire,
   Stood a blue-flag in a bog!

Little flames came wading out,
   Straining, straining towards its stem,
But it was so blue and tall
   That it scorned to think of them!

Red and thirsty were their tongues,
   As the tongues of wolves must be,
But it was so blue and tall—
   Oh, I laughed, I cried, to see!

All my heart became a tear,
   All my soul became a tower,
Never loved I anything
   As I loved that tall blue flower!

It was all the little boats
   That had ever sailed the sea,
It was all the little books
   That had gone to school with me;

On its roots like iron claws
   Rearing up so blue and tall,—
It was all the gallant Earth
   With its back against a wall!

In a breath, ere I had breathed,—
   Oh, I laughed, I cried, to see!—
I was kneeling at its side,
   And it leaned its head on me!

—

Crumbling stones and sliding sand
   Is the road to Heaven now;
Icy at my straining knees
   Drags the awful under-tow;

Soon but stepping-stones of dust
   Will the road to Heaven be, —
Father, Son and Holy Ghost,
   Reach a hand and rescue me!

'There—there, my blue-flag flower;
   Hush—hush—go to sleep;
That is only God you hear,
   Counting up His folded sheep!

Lullabye—lullabye—
   That is only God that calls,
Missing me, seeking me,
   Ere the road to nothing falls!

He will set His mighty feet
   Firmly on the sliding sand;
Like a little frightened bird
   I will creep into His hand;

I will tell Him all my grief,
   I will tell Him all my sin;

He will give me half His robe
    For a cloak to wrap you in.

Lullabye—lullabye—'
    Rocks the burnt-out planet free!—
Father, Son and Holy Ghost,
    Reach a hand and rescue me!

Ah, the voice of love at last!
    Lo, at last the face of light!
And the whole of His white robe
    For a cloak against the night!

And upon my heart asleep
    All the things I ever knew!—
'Holds Heaven not some cranny, Lord,
    For a flower so tall and blue?'

All's well and all's well!
    Gay the lights of Heaven show!
In some moist and Heavenly place
    We will set it out to grow.

SPRING

To what purpose, April, do you return again?
Beauty is not enough.
You can no longer quiet me with the redness
Of little leaves opening stickily.
I know what I know.
The sun is hot on my neck as I observe
The spikes of the crocus.
The smell of the earth is good.
It is apparent that there is no death.
But what does that signify?
Not only under ground are the brains of men
Eaten by maggots.
Life in itself
Is nothing.
An empty cup, a flight of uncarpeted stairs.
It is not enough that yearly, down this hill,
April
Comes like an idiot, babbling and strewing flowers.

EEL-GRASS

No matter what I say,
    All that I really love
Is the rain that flattens on the bay,
    And the eel-grass in the cove;
The jingle shells that lie and bleach
    At the tide-line, and the trace
Of higher tides along the beach:
    Nothing in this place.

EBB

I know what my heart is like
   Since your love died:
It is like a hollow ledge
Holding a little pool
   Left there by the tide,
   A little tepid pool,
Drying inward from the edge.

INLAND

People that build their houses inland,
    People that buy a plot of ground
Shaped like a house, and build a house there,
    Far from the sea-board, far from the sound

Of water sucking the hollow ledges,
    Tons of water striking the shore,—
What do they long for, as I long for
    One salt smell of the sea once more?

People the waves have not awakened,
    Spanking the boats at the harbour's head,
What do they long for, as I long for,—
    Starting up in my inland bed,

Beating the narrow walls, and finding
    Neither a window nor a door,
Screaming to God for death by drowning,—
    One salt taste of the sea once more?

LAMENT

Listen, children:
Your father is dead.
From his old coats
I'll make you little jackets;
I'll make you little trousers
From his old pants.
There'll be in his pockets
Things he used to put there,
Keys and pennies
Covered with tobacco;
Dan shall have the pennies
To save in his bank;
Anne shall have the keys
To make a pretty noise with.
Life must go on,
And the dead be forgotten;
Life must go on,
Though good men die;
Anne, eat your breakfast;
Dan, take your medicine;
Life must go on;
I forget just why.

from MEMORIAL TO D C
(Vassar College, 1918)

II
Prayer to Persephone

Be to her, Persephone,
All the things I might not be;
Take her head upon your knee.
She that was so proud and wild,
Flippant, arrogant and free,
She that had no need of me,
Is a little lonely child
Lost in Hell,—Persephone,
Take her head upon your knee;
Say to her, 'My dear, my dear,
It is not so dreadful here.'

V
Elegy

Let them bury your big eyes
In the secret earth securely,
Your thin fingers, and your fair,
Soft, indefinite-coloured hair,—
All of these, in some way, surely,
From the secret earth shall rise;
Not for these I sit and stare
Broken and bereft completely:
Your young flesh that sat so neatly
On your little bones will sweetly
Blossom in the air.

But your voice… never the rushing
Of a river underground,
Not the rising of the wind
In the trees before the rain,
Not the woodcock's watery call,
Not the note the white-throat utters,
Not the feet of children pushing
Yellow leaves along the gutters
In the blue and bitter fall,
Shall content my musing mind
For the beauty of that sound
That in no new way at all
Ever will be heard again.

Sweetly through the sappy stalk
Of the vigourous weed,
Holding all it held before,
Cherished by the faithful sun,
On and on eternally
Shall your altered fluid run,
Bud and bloom and go to seed:
But your singing days are done;
But the music of your talk
Never shall the chemistry
Of the secret earth restore.
All your lovely words are spoken.
Once the ivory box is broken,
Beats the golden bird no more.

FIRST FIG

My candle burns at both ends;
    It will not last the night;
But ah, my foes, and oh, my friends—
    It gives a lovely light!

SECOND FIG

Safe upon the solid rock the ugly houses stand:
Come and see my shining palace built upon the sand!

RECUERDO

We were very tired, we were very merry—
We had gone back and forth all night on the ferry.
It was bare and bright, and smelled like a stable—
But we looked into a fire, we leaned across a table,
We lay on a hill-top underneath the moon;
And the whistles kept blowing, and the dawn came soon.

We were very tired, we were very merry—
We had gone back and forth all night on the ferry;
And you ate an apple, and I ate a pear,
From a dozen of each we had bought somewhere;
And the sky went wan, and the wind came cold,
And the sun rose dripping, a bucketful of gold.

We were very tired, we were very merry,
We had gone back and forth all night on the ferry.
We hailed, 'Good morrow, mother!' to a shawl-covered head,
And bought a morning paper, which neither of us read;
And she wept, 'God bless you!' for the apples and pears,
And we gave her all our money but our subway fares.

THURSDAY

And if I loved you Wednesday,
    Well, what is that to you?
I do not love you Thursday—
    So much is true.

And why you come complaining
    Is more than I can see.
I loved you Wednesday,—yes—but what
    Is that to me?

What should I be but a prophet and a liar,
Whose mother was a leprechaun, whose father was a friar?
Teethed on a crucifix and cradled under water,
What should I be but the fiend's god-daughter?

And who should be my playmates but the adder and the frog,
That was got beneath a furze-bush and born in a bog?
And what should be my singing, that was christened at an altar,
But Aves and Credos and Psalms out of the Psalter?

You will see such webs on the wet grass, maybe,
As a pixie-mother weaves for her baby,
You will find such flame at the wave's weedy ebb
As flashes in the meshes of a mer-mother's web,

But there comes to birth no common spawn
From the love of a priest for a leprechaun
And you never have seen and you never will see
Such things as the things that swaddled me!

After all's said and after all's done,
What should I be but a harlot and a nun?

In through the bushes, on any foggy day,
My Da would come a-swishing of the drops away,
With a prayer for my death and a groan for my birth,
A-mumbling of his beads for all that he was worth.

And there'd sit my Ma, with her knees beneath her chin,
A-looking in his ace and a-drinking of it in,
And a-marking in the moss some funny little saying
That would mean just the opposite of all that he was praying!

He taught me the holy-talk of Vesper and of Matin,
He heard me my Greek and he heard me my Latin,
He blessed me and crossed me to keep my soul from evil,
And we watched him out of sight, and we conjured up the devil!

Oh, the things I haven't seen and the things I haven't known,
What with hedges and ditches till after I was grown,
And yanked both ways by my mother and my father,
With a 'Which would you better?' and a 'Which would you rather?'

With him for a sire and her for a dam,
What should I be but just what I am?

DAPHNE

Why do you follow me?—
At any moment I can be
Nothing but a laurel-tree.

Any moment of the chase
I can leave you in my place
A pink bough for your embrace.

Yet if over hill and hollow
Still it is your will to follow,
I am off;—to heel, Apollo!

THE DRAGONFLY

I wound myself in a white cocoon of singing,
All day long in the brook's uneven bed.
Measuring out my soul in a mucous thread;
Dimly now to the brook's green bottom clinging,
Men behold me, a worm spun-out and dead,
Walled in an iron house of silky singing.

Nevertheless at length, O reedy shallows,
Not as a plodding nose to the slimy stem,
But as a brazen wing with a spangled hem,
Over the jewel-weed and the pink marshmallows,
Free of these and making a song of them,
I shall arise, and a song of the reedy shallows!

HUMORESQUE

'Heaven bless the babe!' they said.
'What queer books she must have read!'
(Love, by whom I was beguiled,
Grant I may not bear a child.)

'Little does she guess to-day
What the world may be!' they say.
(Snow, drift deep and cover
Till the spring my murdered lover.)

THE BALLAD OF THE HARP-WEAVER

'Son,' said my mother,
   When I was knee-high,
'You've need of clothes to cover you,
   And not a rag have I.

'There's nothing in the house
   To make a boy breeches,
Nor shears to cut a cloth with
   Nor thread to take stitches.

'There's nothing in the house
   But a loaf-end of rye,
And a harp with a woman's head
   Nobody will buy,'
   And she began to cry.

That was in the early fall.
   When came the late fall,
'Son,' she said, 'the sight of you
   Makes your mother's blood crawl,—

'Little skinny shoulder-blades
   Sticking through your clothes!
And where you'll get a jacket from
   God above knows.

'It's lucky for me, lad,
   Your daddy's in the ground,
And can't see the way I let
   His son go around!'
   And she made a queer sound.

That was in the late fall.
    When the winter came,
I'd not a pair of breeches
    Nor a shirt to my name.

I couldn't go to school,
    Or out of doors to play.
And all the other little boys
    Passed our way.

'Son,' said my mother,
    'Come, climb into my lap,
And I'll chafe your little bones
    While you take a nap.'

And, oh, but we were silly
    For half an hour or more,
Me with my long legs
    Dragging on the floor,

A-rock-rock-rocking
    To a mother-goose rhyme!
Oh, but we were happy
    For half an hour's time!

But there was I, a great boy,
    And what would folks say
To hear my mother singing me
    To sleep all day,
    In such a daft way?

Men say the winter
    Was bad that year;
Fuel was scarce,
    And food was dear.

A wind with a wolf's head
  Howled about our door,
And we burned up the chairs
  And sat on the floor.

All that was left us
  Was a chair we couldn't break,
And the harp with a woman's head
  Nobody would take,
  For song or pity's sake.

The night before Christmas
  I cried with the cold,
I cried myself to sleep
  Like a two-year-old.

And in the deep night
  I felt my mother rise,
And stare down upon me
  With love in her eyes.

I saw my mother sitting
  On the one good chair,
A light falling on her
  From I couldn't tell where,

Looking nineteen,
  And not a day older,
And the harp with a woman's head
  Leaned against her shoulder.

Her thin fingers, moving
  In the thin, tall strings,
Were weav-weav-weaving
  Wonderful things.

Many bright threads,
    From where I couldn't see,
Were running through the harp-strings
    Rapidly,

And gold threads whistling
    Through my mother's hand.
I saw the web grow,
    And the pattern expand.

She wove a child's jacket,
    And when it was done
She laid it on the floor
    And wove another one.

She wove a red cloak
    So regal to see,
'She's made it for a king's son,'
    I said, 'and not for me.'
    But I knew it was for me.

She wove a pair of breeches
    Quicker than that!
She wove a pair of boots
    And a little cocked hat.

She wove a pair of mittens,
    She wove a little blouse,
She wove all night
    In the still, cold house.

She sang as she worked,
    And the harp-strings spoke;
Her voice never faltered,
    And the thread never broke.
    And when I awoke,—

There sat my mother
    With the harp against her shoulder
Looking nineteen
    And not a day older,

A smile about her lips,
    And a light about her head,
And her hands in the harp-strings
    Frozen dead.

And piled up beside her
    And toppling to the skies,
Were the clothes of a king's son,
    Just my size.

THE CONCERT

No, I will go alone.
I will come back when it's over.
Yes, of course I love you.
No, it will not be long.
Why may you not come with me?—
You are too much my lover.
You would put yourself
Between me and song.

If I go alone,
Quiet and suavely clothed,
My body will die in its chair,
And over my head a flame,
A mind that is twice my own,
Will mark with icy mirth
The wise advance and retreat
Of armies without a country,
Storming a nameless gate,
Hurling terrible javelins down
From the walls of a singing town
Where no women wait!
Armies clean of love and hate,
Marching lines of pitiless sound
Climbing hills to the sun and hurling
Golden spears to the ground!
Up the lines a silver runner
Bearing a banner whereon is scored
The milk and steel of a bloodless wound
Healed at length by the sword!

You and I have nothing to do with music.
We may not make of music a filigree frame,
Within which you and I,
Tenderly glad we came,
Sit smiling, hand in hand.

Come now, be content.
I will come back to you, I swear I will;
And you will know me still.
I shall be only a little taller
Than when I went.

SIEGE

This I do, being mad:
Gather baubles about me,
Sit in a circle of toys, and all the time
Death beating the door in.

White jade and an orange pitcher,
*   Hindu idol, Chinese god,—*
Maybe next year, when I'm richer—
*   Carved beads and a lotus pod...*

And all this time
Death beating the door in.

SPRING SONG

I know why the yellow forsythia
Holds its breath and will not bloom,
And the robin thrusts his beak in his wing.

Want me to tell you? Think you can bear it?
Cover your eyes with your hand and hear it.
You know how cold the days are still?
And everybody saying how late the Spring is?
Well—cover your eyes with your hand—the thing is,
There isn't going to be any Spring.

No parking here! No parking here!
They said to Spring: No parking here!

Spring came on as she always does,
Laid her hand on the yellow forsythia,—
Little boys turned in their sleep and smiled,
Dreaming of marbles, dreaming of agates;
Little girls leapt from their beds to see
Spring come by with her painted wagons,
Coloured wagons creaking with wonder—

Laid her hand on the robin's throat;
When up comes you-know-who, my dear,
You-know-who in a fine blue coat,
And says to Spring: No parking here!

No parking here! No parking here!
Move on! Move on! No parking here!

Come walk with me in the city gardens.
(Better keep an eye out for you-know-who)
Did you ever see such a sickly showing?—
Middle of June, and nothing growing;
The gardeners peer and scratch their heads
And drop their sweat on the tulip-beds,
But not a blade thrusts through.

Come, move on! Don't you know how to walk?
No parking here! And no back-talk!

Oh, well,—hell, it's all for the best.
She certainly made a lot of clutter,
Dropping petals under the trees,
Taking your mind off your bread and butter.

Anyhow, it's nothing to me.
I can remember, and so can you.
(Though we'd better watch out for you-know-who,
when we sit around remembering Spring).

We shall hardly notice in a year or two.
You can get accustomed to anything.

THE BOBOLINK

Black bird scudding
Under the rainy sky,
How wet your wings must be!
And your small head how sleek and cold with water.

Oh, Bobolink, 'tis you!
Over the buffeted orchard in the summer draught,
Chuckling and singing, charging the rainy cloud,
A little bird gone daft,
A little bird with a secret.

Only the bobolink on the rainy
Rhubarb blossom,
Knows my heart…
For whom adversity has not a word to say that can be heard
Above the din of summer.
The rain has taught us nothing. And the hooves of cattle, and the cat in
   the grass
Have taught us nothing.
The hawk that motionless above the hill
In the pure sky
Stands like a blackened planet
Has taught us nothing,—seeing him shut his wings and fall
Has taught us nothing at all.
In the shadow of the hawk we feather our nests.

Bobolink, you and I, an airy fool and an earthy,
Chuckling under the rain!

I shall never be sad again.
I shall never be sad again.

Ah, sweet, absurd,
Belovèd, bedraggled bird!

Well I remember the pigeons in the sunny arbour
Beyond your open door;
How they conversed throughout the afternoon in their
    monotonous voices never for a moment still;
Always of yesterday they spoke, and of the days before,
Rustling the vine-leaves, twitching the dark shadows of the leaves
    on the bright sill.

You said, the soft curring and droning of the pigeons in the vine
Was a pretty thing enough to the passer-by,
But a maddening thing to the man with his head in his hands,—
    'Like mine! Like mine!'
You said, and ran to the door and waved them off into the sky.

They did not come back. The arbour was empty of their cooing.
The shadows of the leaves were still. 'Whither have they flown,
    then?'
I said, and waited for their wings, but they did not come back. If I
    had known then
What I know now, I never would have left your door.

Tall in your faded smock, with steady hand
Mingling the brilliant pigments, painting your intersecting planes
    you stand,
In a quiet room, empty of the past, of its droning and cooing,
Thinking I know not what, but thinking of me no more,
That left you with a light word, that loving and rueing
Walk in the streets of a city you have never seen,
Walk in a noise of yesterday and of the days before,
Walk in a cloud of wings intolerable, shutting out the sun as if it
    never had been.

THE BUCK IN THE SNOW

White sky, over the hemlocks bowed with snow,
Saw you not at the beginning of evening the antlered buck and his doe
Standing in the apple-orchard? I saw them. I saw them suddenly go,
Tails up, with long leaps lovely and slow,
Over the stone-wall into the wood of hemlocks bowed with snow.

Now lies he here, his wild blood scalding the snow.

How strange a thing is death, bringing to his knees, bringing to his antlers
The buck in the snow.
How strange a thing,—a mile away by now, it may be,
Under the heavy hemlocks that as the moments pass
Shift their loads a little, letting fall a feather of snow—
Life, looking out attentive from the eyes of the doe.

WINE FROM THESE GRAPES

Wine from these grapes I shall be treading surely
Morning and noon and night until I die.
Stained with these grapes I shall lie down to die.

If you would speak with me on any matter,
At any time, come where these grapes are grown;
And you will find me treading them to must.
Lean then above me sagely, lest I spatter
Drops of the wine I tread from grapes and dust.

Stained with these grapes I shall lie down to die.
Three women come to wash me clean
Shall not erase this stain.
Nor leave me lying purely,
Awaiting the black lover.
Death, fumbling to uncover
My body in his bed,
Shall know
There has been one
Before him.

DIRGE WITHOUT MUSIC

I am not resigned to the shutting away of loving hearts in the hard ground.
So it is, and so it will be, for so it has been, time out of mind:
Into the darkness they go, the wise and the lovely. Crowned
With lilies and with laurel they go; but I am not resigned.

Lovers and thinkers, into the earth with you.
Be one with the dull, the indiscriminate dust.
A fragment of what you felt, of what you knew,
A formula, a phrase remains,—but the best is lost.

The answers quick and keen, the honest look, the laughter, the love,— ;
They are gone. They are gone to feed the roses. Elegant and curled
Is the blossom. Fragrant is the blossom. I know. But I do not approve.
More precious was the light in your eyes than all the roses of the world.

Down, down, down into the darkness of the grave
Gently they go, the beautiful, the tender, the kind;
Quietly they go, the intelligent, the witty, the brave.
I know. But I do not approve. And I am not resigned.

THE PLUM GATHERER

The angry nettle and the mild
  Grew together under the blue-plum trees,
I could not tell as a child
  Which was my friend of these.

Always the angry nettle in the skirt of his sister
  Caught my wrist that reached over the ground,
Where alike I gathered,—for the one was sweet and the other wore a
  frosty dust—
  The broken plum and the sound.

The plum-trees are barren now and the black knot is upon them,
  That stood so white in the spring.
I would give, to recall the sweetness and the frost of the lost blue plums,
  Anything, anything.
I thrust my arm among the gray ambiguous nettles, and wait.
  But they do not sting.

Childhood is not from birth to a certain age and at a certain age
The child is grown, and puts away childish things.
Childhood is the kingdom where nobody dies.

Nobody that matters, that is. Distant relatives of course
Die, whom one has never seen or has seen for an hour,
And they gave one candy in a pink-and-green striped bag, or a jack-knife,
And went away, and cannot really be said to have lived at all.

And cats die. They lie on the floor and lash their tails,
And their reticent fur is suddenly all in motion
With fleas that one never knew were there,
Polished and brown, knowing all there is to know,
Trekking off into the living world.
You fetch a shoe-box, but it's much too small, because she won't curl up now:
So you find a bigger box, and bury her in the yard, and weep.
But you do not wake up a month from then, two months,
A year from then, two years, in the middle of the night
And weep, with your knuckles in your mouth, and say Oh, God! Oh, God!
Childhood is the kingdom where nobody dies that matters,—mothers and
    fathers don't die.

And if you have said, 'For heaven's sake, must you always be kissing a person?'
Or, 'I do wish to gracious you'd stop tapping on the window with your
    thimble!'
Tomorrow, or even the day after tomorrow if you're busy having fun,
Is plenty of time to say, 'I'm sorry, mother.'

To be grown up is to sit at the table with people who have died, who neither
    listen nor speak;
Who do not drink their tea, though they always said
Tea was such a comfort.

Run down into the cellar and bring up the last jar of raspberries;
They are not tempted.
Flatter them, ask them what it was they said exactly
That time, to the bishop, or to the overseer, or to Mrs. Mason;
They are not taken in.
Shout at them, get red in the face, rise,
Drag them up out of their chairs by their stiff shoulders and shake them and
    yell at them;
They are not startled, they are not even embarrassed; they slide back into
    their chairs.

Your tea is cold now.
You drink it standing up,
And leave the house.

ON THOUGHT IN HARNESS

My falcon to my wrist
Returns
From no high air.
I sent her toward the sun that burns
Above the mist;
But she has not been there.

Her talons are not cold; her beak
Is closed upon no wonder;
Her head stinks of its hood, her feathers reek
Of me, that quake at the thunder.

Degraded bird, I give you back your eyes forever, ascend now whither you
    are tossed;
Forsake this wrist, forsake this rhyme;
Soar, eat ether, see what has never been seen; depart, be lost,
But climb.

Yet in the end, defeated too, worn out and ready to fall,
Hangs from the drowsy tree with cramped and desperate stem above the
    ditch the last leaf of all.

There is something to be learned, I guess, from looking at the dead leaves
    under the living tree;
Something to be set to a lusty tune and learned and sung, it well might be;
Something to be learned—though I was ever a ten-o' clock scholar at this
    school—
Even perhaps by me.

But my heart goes out to the oak-leaves that are the last to sigh
'Enough' and lose their hold;
They have boasted to the nudging frost and to the two-and-thirty winds
    that they would never die,
Never even grow old.
(These are those russet leaves that cling
All winter, even into the spring,
To the dormant bough, in the wood knee-deep in snow the only coloured
    thing.)

Not for these lovely blooms that prank your chambers did I come. Indeed,
I could have loved you better in the dark;
That is to say, in rooms less bright with roses, rooms more casual, less aware
Of History in the wings about to enter with benevolent air
On ponderous tiptoe, at the cue 'Proceed.'
Not that I like the ash-trays over-crowded and the place in a mess,
Or the monastic cubicle too unctuously austere and stark,
But partly that these formal garlands for our Eighth Street Aphrodite are a
    bit too Greek,
And partly that to make the poor walls rich with our unaided loveliness
Would have been more *chic*.

Yet here I am, having told you of my quarrel with the taxi-driver over a line
    of Milton, and you laugh; and you are you, none other.
Your laughter pelts my skin with small delicious blows.
But I am perverse: I wish you had not scrubbed—with pumice, I suppose—
The tobacco stains from your beautiful fingers. And I wish I did not feel
    like your mother.

THE FITTING

The fitter said, *'Madame, vous avez maigri,'*
And pinched together a handful of skirt at my hip.
'Tant mieux,' I said, and looked away slowly, and took my under-lip
Softly between my teeth.

        Rip—rip!
Out came the seam, and was pinned together in another place.
She knelt before me, a hardworking woman with a familiar and unknown face,
Dressed in linty black, very tight in the arm's-eye and smelling of sweat.
She rose, lifting my arm, and set her cold shears against me,—snip-snip;
Her knuckles gouged my breast. My drooped eyes lifted to my guarded eyes in
    the glass, and glanced away as from someone they had never met.

'Ah, que madame a maigri!' cried the *vendeuse,* coming in with dresses over her
    arm.
'C'est la chaleur,' I said, looking out into the sunny tops of the horse-chestnuts—
    and indeed it was very warm.

I stood for a long time so, looking out into the afternoon, thinking of the
    evening and you...

While they murmured busily in the distance, turning me, touching my secret
    body, doing what they were paid to do.

WHAT SAVAGE BLOSSOM

Do I not know what savage blossom only under the pitting hail
Of your inclement climate could have prospered? Here lie
Green leaves to wade in, and of the many roads not one road leaning
    outward from this place
But is blocked by boughs that will hiss and simmer when they burn—
    green autumn, lady, green autumn on this land!

Do I not know what inward pressure only could inflate its petals to
    withstand
(No, no, not hate, not hate) the onslaught of a little time with you?

No, no, not love, not love. Call it by its name,
Now that it's over, now that it is gone and cannot hear us.

It was an honest thing. Not noble. Yet no shame.

THE PLAID DRESS

Strong sun, that bleach
The curtains of my room, can you not render
Colourless this dress I wear?—
This violent plaid
Of purple angers and red shames; the yellow stripe
Of thin but valid treacheries; the flashy green of kind deeds done
Through indolence, high judgments given in haste;
The recurring checker of the serious breach of taste?

No more uncoloured than unmade,
I fear, can be this garment that I may not doff;
Confession does not strip it off,
To send me homeward eased and bare;

All through the formal, unoffending evening, under the clean
Bright hair,
Lining the subtle gown... it is not seen,
But it is there.

'FONTAINE, JE NE BOIRAI PAS DE TON EAU!'

I know I might have lived in such a way
As to have suffered only pain:
Loving not man nor dog;
Not money, even; feeling
Toothache perhaps, but never more than an hour away
From skill and novocaine;
Making no contacts, dealing with life through agents, drinking one
    cocktail, betting two dollars, wearing raincoats in the rain;
Betrayed at length by no one but the fog
Whispering to the wing of the plane.

'Fountain,' I have cried to that unbubbling well, 'I will not drink of thy
    water!' Yet I thirst
For a mouthful of—not to swallow, only to rinse my mouth in—peace.
    And while the eyes of the past condemn,
The eyes of the present narrow into assignation. And… worst…
The young are so old, they are born with their fingers crossed; I shall get
    no help from them.

I think I will learn some beautiful language, useless for commercial
Purposes, work hard at that.
I think I will learn the Latin name of every songbird, not only in America
  but wherever they sing.
(Shun meditation, though; invite the controversial:
Is the world flat? Do bats eat cats?) By digging hard I might deflect that
  river, my mind, that uncontrollable thing,
Turgid and yellow, strong to overflow its banks in spring, carrying away
  bridges;
A bed of pebbles now, through which there trickles one clear narrow
  stream, following a course henceforth nefast—

Dig, dig; and if I come to ledges, blast.

MODERN DECLARATION

I, having loved ever since I was a child a few things, never having wavered
In these affections; never through shyness in the houses of the rich or in
    the presence of clergymen having denied these loves;
Never when worked upon by cynics like chiropractors having grunted or
    clicked a vertebra to the discredit of those loves;
Never when anxious to land a job having diminished them by a
    conniving smile; or when befuddled by drink
Jeered at them through heartache or lazily fondled the fingers of their
    alert enemies; declare

That I shall love you always.
No matter what party is in power;
No matter what temporarily expedient combination of allied interests
    wins the war;
Shall love you always.

THE TRUE ENCOUNTER

'Wolf!' cried my cunning heart
    At every sheep it spied,
    And roused the countryside.

'Wolf! Wolf!'—and up would start
    Good neighbours, bringing spade
    And pitchfork to my aid.

At length my cry was known:
    Therein lay my release.
I met the wolf alone
    And was devoured in peace.

from TO ELINOR WYLIE
(Died 1928)

II
(1928)

For you there is no song...
    Only the shaking
Of the voice that meant to sing; the sound of the strong
    Voice breaking.

Strange in my hand appears
    The pen, and yours broken.
There are ink and tears on the page; only the tears
    Have spoken.

Intense and terrible, I think, must be the loneliness
Of infants—look at all
The Teddy-bears clasped in slumber in slatted cribs
Painted pale-blue or pink.
And all the Easter Bunnies, dirty and disreputable, that deface
The white pillow and the sterile, immaculate, sunny, turning pleasantly in
    space,
Dainty abode of Baby—try to replace them
With new ones, come Easter again, fluffy and white, and with a different
    smell;
Release with gentle force from the horrified embrace,
That hugs until the stitches give and the stuffing shows,
His only link with a life of his own, the only thing he really knows…
Try to sneak it out of sight.
If you wish to hear anger yell glorious
From air-filled lungs through a throat unthrottled
By what the neighbours will say;

If you wish to witness a human countenance contorted
And convulsed and crumpled by helpless grief and despair,
Then stand beside the slatted crib and say There, there, and take the toy away.

Pink and pale-blue look well
In a nursery. And for the most part Baby is really good:
He gurgles, he whimpers, he tries to get his toe to this mouth; he slobbers his
    food
Dreamily—cereals and vegetable juices—onto his bib:
He behaves as he should.

But do not for a moment believe he has forgotten Blackness; nor the deep
Easy swell; nor his thwarted
Design to remain for ever there;
Nor the crimson betrayal of his birth into a yellow glare.
The pictures painted on the inner eyelids of infants just before they sleep,
Are not in pastel.

Let us go to the Animal Ball, disguised as bipeds!
And the first man down on all fours, pays for the drinks!
Stan has a cocker that can walk on his hind legs, too:
We'll take him along, to support us when the spirit sinks.

We've walked on our hind-legs now so many ages,
We're hoof to the knee, and hock to the hip, but still—
How hot the feet get when you've only two to hit the ground
    with!
It takes real nerve to walk erect, and a pretty strong will.

We went too far when we put on the fur of lynxes,
Of weasels trapped in winter when they've lost their tan;
We went too far when we let the fox assist us
To warm the hide that houses the soul of Man.

The reek of the leopard and the stink of the inky cat
Striped handsomely with white, are in the concert hall;
We sleekly writhe from under them, and are above all that;
But, the concert over, back into our pelts we crawl.

'It is bad to let the dog taste leather.'

By goodness and by evil so surrounded, how can the heart
Maintain a quiet beat?
It races like an idling engine, shaking the whole machine;
And the skin of the inner wrist is blue and green
And yellow, where it has been pounded.

Or else, reluctant to repeat
Bright battles ending always in defeat,
From sadness and discouragement it all but fails;
And the warm blood welling slowly from the weary heart
Before it reaches wrist or temple cools,
Collects in little pools
Along its way, and wishes to remain there, while the face pales,
And diastole and systole meet.

Hair which she still devoutly trusts is red.
Colourless eyes, employing
A childish wonder
To which they have no statistic
Title.
A large mouth,
Lascivious,
Aceticized by blasphemies.
A long throat,
Which will someday
Be strangled.
Thin arms,
In the summer-time leopard
With freckles.
A small body,
Unexclamatory,
But which,
Were it the fashion to wear no clothes,
Would be as well-dressed
As any.

AN ANCIENT GESTURE

I thought, as I wiped my eyes on the corner of my apron:
Penelope did this too.
And more than once: you can't keep weaving all day
And undoing it all through the night;
Your arms get tired, and the back of your neck gets tight;
And along towards morning, when you think it will never be light,
And your husband has been gone, and you don't know where, for years,
Suddenly you burst into tears;
There is simply nothing else to do.

And I thought, as I wiped my eyes on the corner of my apron:
This is an ancient gesture, authentic, antique,
In the very best tradition, classic, Greek;
Ulysses did this too.
But only as a gesture,—a gesture which implied
To the assembled throng that he was much too moved to speak.
He learned it from Penelope...
Penelope, who really cried.

SATIRES

ARIA DA CAPO

PERSONS
Pierrot
Columbine
Cothurnus, Masque of Tragedy
Thyrsis ⎫ *Shepherds*
Corydon ⎭

SCENE: A STAGE

The curtain rises on a stage set for a Harlequinade, a merry black and white interior. Directly behind the footlights, and running parallel with them, is a long table, covered with a gay black and white cloth, on which is spread a banquet. At the opposite ends of this table, seated on delicate thin-legged chairs with high backs, are Pierrot and Columbine, dressed according to the tradition, excepting that Pierrot is in lilac and Columbine in pink. They are dining.

COLUMBINE: Pierrot, a macaroon! I cannot *live* without a macaroon!

PIERROT: My only love,
You are so intense!... Is it Tuesday, Columbine?—
I'll kiss you if it's Tuesday.

COLUMBINE: It is Wednesday,
If you must know... Is this my artichoke,
Or yours?

PIERROT: Ah, Columbine,—as if it mattered!
Wednesday... Will it be Tuesday, then, to-morrow,
By any chance?

COLUMBINE: To-morrow will be—Pierrot,
That isn't funny!

PIERROT: I thought it rather nice.
Well, let us drink some wine and lose our heads
And love each other.

COLUMBINE: Pierrot, don't you love
Me now?

PIERROT: La, what a woman!—how should I know?
Pour me some wine: I'll tell you presently.

COLUMBINE: Pierrot, do you know, I think you drink too
much.

PIERROT: Yes, I dare say I do… Or else too little.
It's hard to tell. You see, I am always wanting
A little more than what I have,—or else
A little less. There's something wrong. My dear,
How many fingers have you?

COLUMBINE: La, indeed,
How should I know?—It always takes me one hand
To count the other with. It's too confusing.
Why?

PIERROT: Why?—I am a student, Columbine;
And search into all matters.

COLUMBINE: La, indeed?—
Count them yourself, then!

PIERROT: No. Or, rather, *nay.*
'Tis of no consequence... I am become
A painter, suddenly,—and you impress me—
Ah, yes!—six orange bull's-eyes, four green pin-wheels,
And one magenta jelly-roll,—the title
As follows: *Woman Taking in Cheese from Fire-Escape.*

COLUMBINE: Well, I like that! So that is all I've meant
To you!

PIERROT: Hush! All at once I am become
A pianist. I will image you in sound...
On a new scale... Without tonality...
Vivace senza tempo senza tutto...
Title: *Uptown Express at Six O'Clock.*
Pour me a drink.

COLUMBINE: Pierrot, you work too hard.
You need a rest. Come on out into the garden,
And sing me something sad.

PIERROT: Don't stand so near me!
I am become a socialist. I love
Humanity; but I hate people. Columbine,
Put on your mittens, child; your hands are cold.

COLUMBINE: My hands are *not* cold!

PIERROT: Oh, I am sure they are.
And you must have a shawl to wrap about you,
And sit by the fire.

COLUMBINE: Why, I'll do no such thing!
I'm hot as a spoon in a teacup!

PIERROT: Columbine,
I'm a philanthropist. I know I am,
Because I feel so restless. Do not scream,
Or it will be the worse for you!

COLUMBINE: Pierrot,
My vinaigrette! I cannot *live* without
My vinaigrette!

PIERROT: My only love, you are
So fundamental!... How would you like to be
An actress, Columbine?—I am become
Your manager.

COLUMBINE: Why, Pierrot, I can't act.

PIERROT: Can't act! Can't act! La, listen to the woman!
What's that to do with the price of furs?—You're blonde,
Are you not?—you have no education, have you?—
Can't act! You underrate yourself, my dear!

COLUMBINE: Yes, I suppose I do.

PIERROT: As for the rest,
I'll teach you how to cry, and how to die,
And other little tricks; and the house will love you.
You'll be a star by five o'clock... that is,
If you will let me pay for your apartment.

COLUMBINE: *Let* you?—well, that's a good one!
Ha! Ha! Ha!
But why?

PIERROT: But why?—well, as to that, my dear,
I cannot say. It's just a matter of form.

COLUMBINE: Pierrot, I'm getting tired of caviar
And peacocks' livers. Isn't there something else
That people eat?—some humble vegetable,
That grows in the ground?

PIERROT: Well, there are mushrooms.

COLUMBINE: Mushrooms!
That's so! I had forgotten… mushrooms… mushrooms…
I cannot *live* with… How do you like this gown?

PIERROT: Not much. I'm tired of gowns that have the waist-
line
About the waist, and the hem around the bottom,—
And women with their breasts in front of them!—
Zut and ehè! Where does one go from here!

COLUMBINE: Here's a persimmon, love. You always liked them.

PIERROT: I am become a critic; there is nothing
I can enjoy… However, set it aside;
I'll eat it between meals.

COLUMBINE: Pierrot, do you know,
Sometimes I think you're making fun of me.

PIERROT: My love, by yon black moon, you wrong us both.

COLUMBINE: There isn't a sign of a moon, Pierrot.

PIERROT: Of course not.
There never was. 'Moon's' just a word to swear by.
'Mutton!'—now *there's* a thing you can lay the hands on,
And set the tooth in! Listen, Columbine:
I always lied about the moon and you.
Food is my only lust.

COLUMBINE: Well, eat it, then,
For Heaven's sake, and stop your silly noise!
I haven't heard the clock tick for an hour.

PIERROT: It's ticking all the same. If you were a fly,
You would be dead by now. And if I were a parrot,
I could be talking for a thousand years!

(Enter Cothurnus.)

PIERROT: Hello, what's this, for God's sake?— What's the
matter?
Say, whadda you mean?—get off the stage, my friend,
And pinch yourself,—you're walking in your sleep!

COTHURNUS: I never sleep.

PIERROT: Well, anyhow, clear out.
You don't belong on here. Wait for your own scene!
Whadda you think this is,—a dress-rehearsal?

COTHURNUS: Sir, I am tired of waiting. I will wait
No longer.

PIERROT: Well, but whadda you going to do?
The scene is set for me!

COTHURNUS: True, sir; yet I
Can play the scene.

PIERROT: Your scene is down for later!

COTHURNUS: That, too, is true, sir; but I play it now.

PIERROT: Oh, very well!—Anyway, I am tired
Of black and white. At least, I think I am.

(Exit Columbine.)

Yes, I am sure I am. I know what I'll do!—
I'll go and strum the moon, that's what I'll do...
Unless, perhaps... you never can tell... I may be,
You know, tired of the moon. Well, anyway,
I'll go find Columbine... And when I find her,
I will address her thus: *'Ehè, Pierrette!'*—
There's something in that.

(Exit Pierrot.)

COTHURNUS: You, Thyrsis! Corydon!
Where are you?

THYRSIS: *(Off stage.)* Sir, we are in our dressing-room!

COTHURNUS: Come out and do the scene.

CORYDON: *(Off stage.)* You are mocking us!—
The scene is down for later.

COTHURNUS: That is true;
But we will play it now. I am the scene.

(Seats himself on high place in back of stage.)

(Enter Corydon and Thyrsis.)

CORYDON: Sir, we are counting on this little hour.
We said, 'Here is an hour,—in which to think
A mighty thought, and sing a trifling song,
And look at nothing.'—And, behold! the hour,
Even as we spoke, was over, and the act begun,
Under our feet!

THYRSIS: Sir, we are not in the fancy
To play the play. We had thought to play it later.

CORYDON: Besides, this is the setting for a farce.
Our scene requires a wall; we cannot build
A wall of tissue-paper!

THYRSIS: We cannot act
A tragedy with comic properties!

COTHURNUS: Try it and see. I think you'll find you can.
One wall is like another. And regarding
The matter of your insufficient mood,
The important thing is that you speak the lines,
And make the gestures. Wherefore I shall remain
Throughout, and hold the prompt-book. Are you ready?

CORYDON-THYRSIS: *(Sorrowfully.)* Sir, we are always ready.

COTHURNUS: Play the play!

(Corydon and Thyrsis move the table and chairs to one side out of the way, and seat themselves in a half-reclining position on the floor.)

THYRSIS: How gently in the silence, Corydon,
Our sheep go up the bank. They crop a grass
That's yellow where the sun is out, and black
Where the clouds drag their shadows. Have you noticed
How steadily, yet with what a slanting eye
They graze?

CORYDON: As if they thought of other things.
What say you, Thyrsis, do they only question
Where next to pull?—Or do their far minds draw them
Thus vaguely north of west and south of east?

THYRSIS: One cannot say… The black lamb wears its burdocks
As if they were a garland,—have you noticed?
Purple and white—and drinks the bitten grass
As if it were a wine.

CORYDON: I've noticed that.
What say you, Thyrsis, shall we make a song
About a lamb that thought himself a shepherd?

THYRSIS: Why, yes!—that is, why,—no. (I have forgotten my
line.)

COTHURNUS: *(Prompting.)* 'I know a game worth two of that!'

THYRSIS: Oh, yes… I know a game worth two of that!
Let's gather rocks, and build a wall between us;
And say that over there belongs to me,
And over here to you!

CORYDON: Why,—very well.
And say you may not come upon my side
Unless I say you may!

THYRSIS: Nor you on mine!
And if you should, 'twould be the worse for you!

(They weave a wall of coloured crêpe paper ribbons from the centre front to the centre back of the stage, fastening the ends to Columbine's chair in front and to Pierrot's chair in the back.)

CORYDON: Now there's a wall a man may see across,
But not attempt to scale.

THYRSIS: An excellent wall.

CORYDON: Come, let us separate, and sit alone
A little while, and lay a plot whereby
We may outdo each other.

(They seat themselves on opposite sides of the wall.)

PIERROT: *(Off stage.)*   *Ehè*, Pierrette!

COLUMBINE: *(Off stage.)* My name is Columbine! Leave me
alone!

THYRSIS: *(Coming up to the wall.)* Corydon, after all, and in
spite of the fact
I started it myself, I do not like this
So very much. What is the sense of saying
I do not want you on my side the wall?
It is a silly game. I'd much prefer
Making the little song you spoke of making,
About the lamb, you know, that thought himself
A shepherd!—what do you say?

(Pause.)

CORYDON: *(At wall.)* I have forgotten the line.

COTHURNUS: *(Prompting.)* 'How do I know this isn't a
trick—'

CORYDON: Oh, yes... How do I know this isn't a trick
To get upon my land?

THYRSIS: Oh, Corydon,
You *know* it's not a trick. I do not like
The game, that's all. Come over here, or let me
Come over there.

CORYDON: It is a clever trick
To get upon my land. *(Seats himself as before.)*

THYRSIS: Oh, very well! *(Seats himself as
before.)*
(To himself.) I think I never knew a sillier game.

CORYDON: *(Coming to wall.)* Oh, Thyrsis, just a minute!—all
the water
Is on your side the wall, and the sheep are thirsty.
I hadn't thought of that.

THYRSIS: Oh, hadn't you?

CORYDON: Why, what do you mean?

THYRSIS: What do I mean?—I mean
That I can play a game as well as you can.
And if the pool is on my side, it's on
My side, that's all.

CORYDON: You mean you'd let the sheep
Go thirsty?

THYRSIS: Well, they're not my sheep. My sheep
Have water enough.

CORYDON: *Your* sheep! You are mad, to call them
Yours—mine—they are all one flock! Thyrsis, you can't mean
To keep the water from them, just because
They happened to be grazing over here
Instead of over there, when we set the wall up?

THYRSIS: Oh, can't I?—wait and see!—and if you try
To lead them over here, you'll wish you hadn't!

CORYDON: I wonder how it happens all the water
Is on your side… I'll say you had an eye out
For lots of little things, my innocent friend,
When I said, 'Let us make a song,' and you said,
'I know a game worth two of that!'

COLUMBINE: *(Off stage.)*   Pierrot,
D'you know, I think you must be getting old,
Or fat, or something,—stupid, anyway!—
Can't you put on some other kind of collar?

THYRSIS: You know as well as I do, Corydon,
I never thought anything of the kind.
Don't you?

CORYDON: I *do* not.

THYRSIS: Don't you?

CORYDON: Oh, I suppose so.
Thyrsis, let's drop this,—what do you say?—it's only
A game, you know... we seem to be forgetting
It's only a game... a pretty serious game
It's getting to be, when one of us is willing
To let the sheep go thirsty for the sake of it.

THYRSIS: I know it, Corydon.

(They reach out their arms to each other across the wall.)

COTHURNUS: *(Prompting.)* 'But how do I know—'

THYRSIS: Oh, yes... But how do I know this isn't a trick
To water your sheep, and get the laugh on me?

CORYDON: You can't know, that's the difficult thing about it,
Of course,—you can't be sure. You have to take
My word for it. And I know just how you feel.
But one of us has to take a risk, or else,
Why, don't you see?—the game goes on forever!...
It's terrible, when you stop to think of it...
Oh, Thyrsis, now for the first time I feel
This wall is actually a wall, a thing
Come up between us, shutting you away
From me... I do not know you any more!

THYRSIS: No, don't say that! Oh, Corydon, I'm willing
To drop it all, if you will! Come on over
And water your sheep! It is an ugly game.
I hated it from the first... How did it start?

CORYDON: I do not know... I do not know... I think
I am afraid of you!—you are a stranger!

I never set eyes on you before! 'Come over
And water my sheep,' indeed!—They'll be more thirsty
Than they are now before I bring them over
Into your land, and have you mixing them up
With yours, and calling them yours, and trying to keep them!

(Enter Columbine)

COLUMBINE: *(To Cothurnus.)* Glummy, I want my hat.

THYRSIS: Take it, and go.

COLUMBINE: Take it and go, indeed. Is it my hat,
Or isn't it? Is this my scene, or not?
Take it and go! Really, you know, you two
Are awfully funny!

(Exit Columbine)

THYRSIS: Corydon, my friend,
I'm going to leave you now, and whittle me
A pipe, or sing a song, or go to sleep.
When you have come to your senses, let me know.

*(Goes back to where he has been sitting, lies down and sleeps.
Corydon, in going back to where he has been sitting, stumbles over
bowl of coloured confetti and coloured paper ribbons.)*

CORYDON: Why, what is this?—Red stones—and purple
stones—
And stones stuck full of gold!—The ground is full
Of gold and coloured stones!... I'm glad the wall
Was up before I found them!—Otherwise,
I should have had to share them. As it is,
They all belong to me... Unless—

(He goes to wall and digs up and down the length of it, to see if there are jewels on the other side.)

                          None here—
None here—none here—They all belong to me! *(Sits.)*

THYRSIS: *(Awakening.)* How curious! I thought the little black lamb
Came up and licked my hair; I saw the wool
About its neck as plain as anything!
It must have been a dream. The little black lamb
Is on the other side of the wall, I'm sure.

(Goes to wall and looks over. Corydon is seated on the ground, tossing the confetti up into the air and catching it.)

Hello, what's that you've got there, Corydon?

CORYDON: Jewels.

THYRSIS: Jewels?—And where did you ever get them?

CORYDON: Oh, over here.

THYRSIS: You mean to say you found them,
By digging around in the ground for them?

CORYDON: *(Unpleasantly.)*   No, Thyrsis,
By digging down for water for my sheep.

THYRSIS: Corydon, come to the wall a minute, will you?
I want to talk to you.

CORYDON: I haven't time.
I'm making me a necklace of red stones.

THYRSIS: I'll give you all the water that you want,
For one of those red stones,—if it's a good one.

CORYDON: Water?—what for?—what do I want of water?

THYRSIS: Why, for your sheep!

CORYDON: My sheep?—I'm not a shepherd!

THYRSIS: Your sheep are dying of thirst.

CORYDON: Man, haven't I told you
I can't be bothered with a few untidy
Brown sheep all full of burdocks?—I'm a merchant.
That's what I am!—And if I set my mind to it
I dare say I could be an emperor!
(To himself.) Wouldn't I be a fool to spend my time
Watching a flock of sheep go up a hill,
When I have these to play with?—when I have these
To think about?—I can't make up my mind
Whether to buy a city, and have a thousand
Beautiful girls to bathe me, and be happy
Until I die, or build a bridge, and name it
The Bridge of Corydon,—and be remembered
After I'm dead.

THYRSIS: Corydon, come to the wall,
Won't you?—I want to tell you something.

CORYDON: Hush!
Be off! Be off! Go finish your nap, I tell you!

THYRSIS: Corydon, listen: if you don't want your sheep,
Give them to me.

CORYDON: Be off! Go finish your nap.
A red one—and a blue one—and a red one—
And a purple one—give you my sheep, did you say?—
Come, come! What do you take me for, a fool?
I've a lot of thinking to do,—and while I'm thinking,
The sheep might just as well be over here
As over there… A blue one—and a red one—

THYRSIS: But they will die!

CORYDON: And a green one—and a couple
Of white ones, for a change.

THYRSIS: Maybe I have
Some jewels on my side.

CORYDON: And another green one—
Maybe, but I don't think so. You see, this rock
Isn't so very wide. It stops before
It gets to the wall. It seems to go quite deep,
However.

THYRSIS: *(With hatred.)* I see.

COLUMBINE: *(Off stage.)* Look, Pierrot, there's the moon.

PIERROT: *(Off stage.)* Nonsense!

THYRSIS: I see.

COLUMBINE: *(Off stage.)* Sing me an old song, Pierrot,—
Something I can remember.

PIERROT: *(Off stage.)*　　　　　Columbine,
Your mind is made of crumbs,—like an escallop
Of oysters,—first a layer of crumbs, and then
An oystery taste, and then a layer of crumbs.

THYRSIS: *(Searching.)* I find no jewels... but I wonder what
The root of this black weed would do to a man
If he should taste it... I have seen a sheep die,
With half the stalk still drooling from its mouth.
'Twould be a speedy remedy, I should think,
For a festered pride and a feverish ambition.
It has a curious root. I think I'll hack it
In little pieces... First I'll get me a drink;
And then I'll hack that root in little pieces
As small as dust, and see what the colour is
Inside. *(Goes to bowl on floor.)*

　　　　The pool is very clear. I see
A shepherd standing on the brink, with a red cloak
About him, and a black weed in his hand...
'Tis I. *(Kneels and drinks.)*

CORYDON: *(Coming to wall.)* Hello, what are you doing,
Thyrsis?

THYRSIS: Digging for gold.

CORYDON:　　　　　　　　I'll give you all the gold
You want, if you'll give me a bowl of water.
If you don't want too much, that is to say.

THYRSIS: Ho, so you've changed your mind?—It's different,
Isn't it, when you want a drink yourself?

CORYDON: Of course it is.

THYRSIS: Well, let me see... a bowl
Of water,—come back in an hour, Corydon.
I'm busy now.

CORYDON: Oh, Thyrsis, give me a bowl
Of water!—and I'll fill the bowl with jewels,
And bring it back!

THYRSIS: Be off, I'm busy now.

(He catches sight of the weed, picks it up and looks at it, unseen by Corydon.)

Wait!—Pick me out the finest stones you have...
I'll bring you a drink of water presently.

CORYDON: *(Goes back and sits down, with the jewels before him.)* A bowl of jewels is a lot of jewels.

THYRSIS: *(Chopping up the weed.)* I wonder if it has a bitter taste.

CORYDON: There's sure to be a stone or two among them
I have grown fond of, pouring them from one hand
Into the other.

THYRSIS: I hope it doesn't taste
Too bitter, just at first.

CORYDON: A bowl of jewels
Is far too many jewels to give away
And not get back again.

THYRSIS: I don't believe
He'll notice. He's too thirsty. He'll gulp it down
And never notice.

CORYDON: There ought to be some way
To get them back again... I could give him a necklace,
And snatch it back, after I'd drunk the water,
I suppose... Why, as for that, of course a *necklace*...

(He puts two or three of the coloured tapes together and tries their strength by pulling them, after which he puts them around his neck and pulls them, gently, nodding to himself. He gets up and goes to the wall, with the coloured tapes in his hands.)

(THYRSIS in the meantime has poured the powdered root—black confetti—into the pot which contained the flower and filled it up with wine from the punch-bowl on the floor. He comes to the wall at the same time, holding the bowl of poison.)

THYRSIS: Come, get your bowl of water, Corydon.

CORYDON: Ah, very good!—and for such a gift as that
I'll give you more than a bowl of unset stones.
I'll give you three long necklaces, my friend.
Come closer. Here they are. *(Puts the ribbons about Thyrsis' neck.)*

THYRSIS: *(Putting bowl to Corydon's mouth.)* I'll hold the bowl
Until you've drunk it all.

CORYDON: Then hold it steady.
For every drop you spill I'll have a stone back
Out of this chain.

THYRSIS: I shall not spill a drop.

(Corydon drinks, meanwhile beginning to strangle Thyrsis.)

THYRSIS: Don't pull the string so tight.

CORYDON: You're spilling the water.

THYRSIS: You've had enough—you've had enough—stop pulling
The string so tight!

CORYDON: Why, that's not tight at all...
How's this?

THYRSIS: *(Drops bowl.)* You're strangling me! Oh,
Corydon! It's only a game!—and you are strangling me!

CORYDON: It's only a game, is it?—Yet I believe
You've poisoned me in earnest! *(Writhes and pulls the strings
tighter, winding them about Thyrsis' neck.)*

THYRSIS: Corydon! *(Dies.)*

CORYDON: You've poisoned me in earnest... I feel so cold...
So cold... this is a very silly game...
Why do we play it?—let's not play this game
A minute more... let's make a little song
About a lamb... I'm coming over the wall,
No matter what you say,—I want to be near you...

*(Groping his way, with arms wide before him, he strides through
the frail papers of the wall without knowing it, and continues
seeking for the wall straight across the stage.)*

Where is the wall?

(*Gropes his way back, and stands very near Thyrsis without seeing him; he speaks slowly.*)

There isn't any wall, I think.

(*Takes a step forward, his foot touches Thyrsis' body, and he falls down beside him.*)

Thyrsis, where is your cloak?—just give me
A little bit of your cloak!...

(*Draws corner of Thyrsis' cloak over his shoulders, falls across Thyrsis' body, and dies. Cothurnus closes the prompt-book with a bang, arises matter-of-factly, comes down stage, and places the table over the two bodies, drawing down the cover so that they are hidden from any actors on the stage, but visible to the audience, pushing in their feet and hands with his boot. He then turns his back to the audience, and claps his hands twice.*)

COTHURNUS: Strike the scene!

(*Exit Cothurnus. Enter Pierrot and Columbine.*)

PIERROT: Don't puff so, Columbine!

COLUMBINE: Lord, what a mess
This set is in! If there's one thing I hate
Above everything else,—even more than getting my feet wet—
It's clutter!—He might at least have left the scene
The way he found it... don't you say so, Pierrot?

(*She picks up punch bowl. They arrange chairs as before at ends of table.*)

PIERROT: Well, I don't know. I think it rather diverting
The way it is. *(Yawns, picks up confetti bowl.)*

Shall we begin?

COLUMBINE: *(Screams.)*   My God!
What's that there under the table?

PIERROT: It is the bodies
Of the two shepherds from the other play.

COLUMBINE: *(Slowly.)* How curious to strangle him like that,
With coloured paper ribbons.

PIERROT: Yes, and yet
I dare say he is just as dead. *(Pauses. Calls.)* Cothurnus!
Come drag these bodies out of here! We can't
Sit down and eat with two dead bodies lying
Under the table!... The audience wouldn't stand for it!

COTHURNUS: *(Off stage.)* What makes you think so?—Pull
down the tablecloth
On the other side, and hide them from the house,
And play the farce. The audience will forget.

PIERROT: That's so. Give me a hand there, Columbine.

*(Pierrot and Columbine pull down the table cover in such a way
that the two bodies are hidden from the house, then merrily set
their bowls back on the table, draw up their chairs, and begin the
play exactly as before.)*

COLUMBINE: Pierrot, a macaroon,—I cannot *live*
Without a macaroon!

PIERROT: My only love,
You are *so* intense!… Is it Tuesday, Columbine?—
I'll kiss you if it's Tuesday.

(Curtains begin to close slowly.)

COLUMBINE: It is Wednesday,
If you must know… Is this my artichoke
Or yours?

PIERROT: Ah, Columbine, as if it mattered!
Wednesday… Will it be Tuesday, then, to-morrow,
By any chance?…

(Curtain.)

from DISTRESSING DIALOGUES
by Nancy Boyd

Preface

Miss Boyd has asked me to write a preface to these dialogues, with which, having followed them eagerly as they appeared from time to time in the pages of Vanity Fair, I was already familiar. I am no friend of prefaces, but if there must be one to this book, it should come from me, who was its author's earliest admirer. I take pleasure in recommending to the public these excellent small satires, from the pen of one in whose work I have a never-failing interest and delight.

EDNA ST VINCENT MILLAY
Tokyo, May 6, 1924

Scene: *A studied studio, in which nine o'clock tea and things are being served by Miss Black, a graceful sculptress, to Mr. White, a man of parts, but badly assembled. Miss Black is tattooed with batik; Mr. White is as impeccably attired for the evening as a professional violinist.*

H E : My dear Miss Black, you are, if you will permit me to say so, the most interesting unmarried woman of my acquaintance.

S H E (*languidly flicking an ash from a cigarette-holder the approximate length of a fencing-foil*): Oh, yes?

H E : Yes. You are the only unmarried woman I know with whom I find it possible to talk freely on any subject. (*He clears his throat.*)

S H E (*gazing at him with clear, straightforward eyes*): You interest me. (*She waits for him to continue.*)

H E (*continuing*): You have such an intrepid mind, I feel, so unblenched a vision. The petty concerns that make up the lives of other people, they are not your life. You see beyond their little disputes, their little aspirations, their little loves, into a world, a cosmos, where men and women can understand each other, can help each other, where the barriers of sex are like a mist in the air, dissipated with the dawn.

S H E (*cosmically*): It is true that for me there are no barriers.

H E (*almost with excitement*): I know that! I know that! And that is how I know that you mean what you say—for the very simple reason that you are not afraid to say what you mean—and that at this moment, for example, as you sit there, so beautiful, so more than beautiful, talking to me like a soul detached, a soul freed of the earth,—you are not all the time considering just how long it will take you to get me to propose to you! (*She starts and blushes a little, but he goes on without noticing.*) Oh, if you only knew what a relief you are, what a rest!—a woman who is not married, who has never been married, and who does not insist that I marry her. Please do not think me boastful. It is not that I am so very attractive. I dare say it is the experience of every eligible man. And doubtless when they have had a good look at me, they decide against me. But unmarried women always give me the uncomfortable feeling that they are looking me over; and I object to being looked over, with matrimony a forethought.

SHE (*sympathetically*): I know. But I am sorry for them. They have nothing else with which to occupy their minds. That I am different from these women is through no virtue of my own, but only because I am blessed with a talent which releases my spirit into other channels. Whether the talent be great or small (*she deprecates gracefully toward the clutter of statuary about the studio*) is of no consequence. It is sufficient to ease my need.

HE (*following the direction of her gesture, and considering the reclining figure of a nymph on a table beside him*): What a charming study! Such subtle lines, such exquisite proportions. Who is she?

SHE: I call her Daphne. She was running, you see,—and has fallen.

HE: Oh. But I mean to say, who is your model? You are fortunate to have found a creature at once so delicate and so roundly contoured.

SHE: Oh.

(*There is an appreciable pause.*)

SHE (*frankly*): Why, you see, I *have* no model. They are so difficult to get, and they are mostly so bad. I—am my own model. You notice the two long mirrors?—I place the stand between them, and work from my reflections.

(*There is an appreciable pause.*)

HE (*pulling down his coat-sleeves over his cuffs, and adjusting his tie*): What an interesting idea.

SHE (*laughing gaily*): Yes—and so economical!

(*She rises and lights the alcohol lamp under a small brass tea-kettle. Her heavy, loose robe clings to her supple limbs. The flame sputters. With an impatient exclamation she drops to her knees and considers the lamp from beneath, with critical attention. The sleeves fall back from her lifted arms; her fine brows scowl a little; her vermilion lips are pouted in concentration.*)

HE (*with ponderous lightness*): Miss Black, I dare say that to many of my sex you are a dangerously attractive woman.

SHE (*rising sinuously, and dusting her hands, which seem to caress each other*): Well,—yes. In fact (*smiling faintly*), you are the only man in my acquaintance, unmarried or married, who does not importune me with undesirable attentions.

HE (*with aesthetic ferocity*): Of course. I know how it is. They don't see you as I do. They do not desire to leave you free, as I do. They don't know what you are. It is your beauty which attracts them, your extraordinary grace, your voice, so thrillingly quiet, your ravishing gestures. They don't see you as I do. (*He is silent, breathing hard.*)

SHE (*in a burst of confidence*): It is true. I don't know what it is about me, but I am besieged by suitors. I have not a moment to myself. All day long, all day long, the bell rings; I open the door; they drop on their knees; I tell them not to be absurd; they insist upon giving me their hearts; I insist that I have no room for anything more in my apartment! they arise, dust their trousers, curse my beauty, gulp, yank open the door,—and the bell rings. You alone, of them all, see me as I am. You know that I am not beautiful, you are undisturbed by my proximity, it is possible for me to talk with you, as—as one star talks to another. (*She leans back wearily and closes her eyes, exposing a long and treacherous throat, full of memories.*)

HE (*a little uncertainly*): Well—I—it is true that I—er—admire you for your true worth, that I really appreciate you, and that your external attributes have nothing to do with that appreciation. But it would be impossible for any man, who could be called a man, to be blind to your incredible charm, your inscrutable, unconscious fascination. For I know it is unconscious,—you are lovely as a flower is lovely, without effort. I am aware of all this, although, as you say, I am unmoved by it.

(*She turns her head slowly, and opens upon him a pair of wondering, topaz eyes. He swallows audibly, but meets the look without flinching.*)

HE (*stoutly*): What does move me, and to what extent you cannot possibly imagine (*he shifts convulsively in his chair*), is your unparalleled genius, the poise and vigour of your work. I want you to go on—to grow—to grow—and to be free!

SHE (*tensely*): I *must* be free. I must.

HE: I know. And if there is anything I can do to make you freer—

SHE: I know. I know. (*Selecting a cigarette from the lacquer tray at her elbow, she thoughtfully twists it into her cigarette-holder.*) I am sorry that you think me beautiful. But I suppose it cannot be helped. (*She sighs.*) You must forgive me, but I am always a little sorry when a man becomes even conscious of me as a woman. Nothing may come of it, of course,—in this instance, I am sure, nothing will— (*She flashes at him a little candid smile.*) But there is always the danger, for we are, among other things, human beings, and—oh, I am troubled that you said that! (*She twists her long hands; her jade rings click together.*)

HE (*sitting forward on his chair and taking her restless fingers firmly in his trembling hands*): Have no fear of me. Believe me, if it came to that, I should go. You should never guess. Rather than hurt you, I should go. I should get up and go, suddenly, without even saying good-bye, and you would never guess.

SHE (*smiling a little lonely smile*): I know. I know you would. You are like that.

HE (*intensely*): I would do anything rather than hurt you in the slightest degree,—so high do I rate your talent.

SHE: I know. (*She leans back her head and closes her eyes.*) It is good to feel that I have your friendship. I have so little—friendship.

HE (*thickly, staring at her pained and perfect mouth*): You will have my friendship always, as long as you want it. And even when you tire of me, and don't want it any more, you will still have it. Remember that. Woman though you are, you stir me more deeply by your genius than ever a man has done. (*He bows his head on her hands.*)

SHE (*looking thoughtfully down at the top of his head*): You are so kind, so kind to be distressed for my sake. Please don't be distressed. Come let's have our tea. I am really all right, you know. It's just that, at times, I am a little sad.

HE (*lifting his head and looking into her sad eyes*): Yes, you are sad. And I am sad, too. How curious that we should both be sad! If only I could do something to comfort you. Please don't look like that.

SHE (*with a gay smile that is obviously a little forced*): Very well! There now!—I am quite happy again, you see! Come, let's have our tea.

(*He sits back in his chair, and looks curiously at the arms of it, feeling that he has been away a long time. She busies herself with the tea things.*)

SHE (*after a moment, peering into the black and silver Chinese tea-pot*): Do you know, it's extraordinary, the way I feel about tea: I have to have it. It's the one thing I couldn't possibly get along without. Money, clothes, books, mirrors, friends—all these I could dispense with. But tea,—I have to have it. Fortunately, its connotation, as being the accomplice of spinsterhood, is not so offensive to me as it is to most women. If it will help me to remain a spinster, then it is my staunchest ally! (*She laughs gaily.*)

HE (*wincing, but recovering himself*): I'm just that way about my pipe. (*Suddenly remembering his pipe, he gropes for it pitifully, as for the hand of a comrade in the dark. But it occurs to him that she probably objects to pipe-smoke. He withdraws his hand from his pocket, sighing.*)

S H E (*without looking up*): Why don't you smoke your pipe?

H E (*incredulously*): Wouldn't it annoy you?

S H E: Heavens, no!

(*He draws his pipe from his pocket and fills it, gratefully, meanwhile watching her. She is cruelly slicing a lemon, by means of a small dagger with which a Castilian nun has slain three matadors; it strikes him that she looks gentle and domestic. A great peace steals over him.*)

H E (*contentedly*): What a pleasant room this is.

S H E (*delicately poising in her hand a sugar-tongs made from the hind claws of a baby gila-monster, and glancing lovingly about the room*): Yes. It breaks my heart that I have to leave it. Two lumps, or three?

H E: Have to leave it? Er—no, thanks, I don't like tea—well, three lumps—have to *leave* it? (*He grasps his cup and saucer and holds them before him, as if they were an unfamiliar pair of infant twins.*)

S H E: Yes. You see (*conversationally*), I'm sailing for Europe on the fifteenth, and—

H E (*hoarsely*): Fifteenth of what? (*His cup and saucer rattle together now like a pair of dice.*)

SHE (*pleasantly*): Fifteenth of this month. It will be of infinite value to me in my work, I am sure,—and I think only of that. Yet I hate to leave these rooms. I've been here—

HE: Don't—don't—don't talk—be quiet—Oh, God—let me think! (*With awful care he deposits his cup and saucer on the table at his elbow. She watches him intently.*)

HE (*suddenly sliding from his chair to the floor and kneeling before her*): But what about me? What about me?

SHE (*coldly*): I don't understand you.

HE: You say you're going because it will help your work,—but think of me! What will happen to me?

SHE: I'm sure I don't know. It hadn't occurred to me to consider.

HE (*shouting*): No! Of course not! Oh, you're cold, you are—and cruel, my God! Your work! (*He laughs scornfully.*) All you think about is those damn little putty figures. And here am I, flesh and blood,—and what do you care?

SHE (*icily*): Less and less.

HE (*groaning*): And you can say that—and me loving you the way I do! You don't mean it! Oh, if you'd only marry me, I'd make you care. I'd make you so happy!

SHE (*with revulsion*): Oh, really,—I must *ask* you—

HE: I don't care how much you work—work your head off! A man's wife *ought* to have some little thing to take up her time. But as for—oh, Lord—(*He buries his face in the folds of her gown.*) *What* am I going to do?

(*She has no suggestions to offer.*)

HE (*abruptly rising and glaring down at her*): Do you know what I think?—I think you're enjoying this! I think it's the breath of life to you!

SHE (*earnestly*): No, really. I assure you—I am frightfully distressed—I had no idea you felt like this—I—

HE (*wildly*): You're a lying woman!

SHE (*rising, white with the fury of the righteous unjustly accused*): Will you be so good as to go?

HE (*laughing boisterously, then in a subdued and hopeless voice*): Very well. Of course I'll go if you want me to. But my heart I leave here.

SHE (*languidly*): Pray don't. I have room for nothing more in the apartment.

(*With a growl he yanks open the door and leaps forth, slamming it behind him. She goes to the table and pours herself a cup of cold tea.*)

SHE (*after a moment of silence, running her jaded fingers through her hair*): Oh, dear, I *wish* I were not so restless!

(*Curtain.*)

My days, gentle reader, are a headlong flight before the onrushing hordes of the socially-minded.

I flee from border to border, from rural fastness to urban looseness.

I gather no moss.

No grass, not even a mushroom, grows under my feet.

I am seeking a place where I may be alone.

With the money I have expended in keeping my passport in order, I could have bought myself a nice little house just like everybody else's nice little house in Pelham Pay.

I have preferred to collect visas.

And Pelham Bay has turned out as one man, checked its croquet-set, laid straw at the roots of its Dorothy Perkins, and followed the mark of my French heel in the mud through fourteen countries and into the jaws of Monte Carlo.

Why people should pursue me, no one knows.

I am neither rich nor beautiful.

I have stolen no jewels, kidnapped no babies, founded no religion, built no mouse-traps.

I have simply made the mistake of starting to run. And everybody is chasing me.

I am a hen that has scuttled to a distant corner of the barnyard in order that she may be hungry by herself.

And every hen for farms around is convinced I have a kernel of corn.

Most people, I have noted in passing, observing them as I do fleetingly from the decks of steamers, from the platforms of trains, from behind lamp-posts, around corners and through thick veils, are afraid to be alone in the dark.

They are always forming themselves into clubs.

In order that they may smoke together.

Drink together.

Narrate improprieties together.

Look out of windows at taxis together.

And grow bald together.

They imagine that the volume of fatigue and the avoirdupois of doom become in this way divided by the number of the club's membership.

And that no member receives more than he can nicely bear.

As for me, I was never a joiner.

The feeling which stirs a mob to applause, to derision, to violence or to tears, stirs me only to uneasiness of the alimentary canal.

Over me, no less than another, bend the malign forces of Providence.

But I may honestly say that I fear no catastrophe save that of the companionship of tiresome people. I refuse to be one of a group.

It chafes me when people say, comprising me in their remark, 'Us Americans.'

It rubs me when women, recruiting me by their glance, declaim, 'We women feel—'

It irks me even that I have a life membership in that degenerate sporting-club known as the Human Race.

Persons are constantly making the mistake of supposing that just because they once lived in the same street, because they both are strangers in a foreign capital, because they have attended the same Keeley-Cure, or because they have married the same woman, they must perforce have a world of things in common.

As a matter of fact, most people have nothing at all in common, beyond that cold perspiration budding from the strong man's brow at the thought that some day or other he may find himself spending a half-hour alone.

For my part, I fail to feel necessarily a choking surge of

affection for the butcher, the baker, the gas-fixture-maker who happened to buy the house next-door to the house I rented.

For the Belgian who, at the time of his birth, chanced to be traveling with his mother in my home town.

Or for the forty thousand or so estimable and active women who received their degrees at the university from which I was at one time expelled.

I wish them no harm.

I merely desire that they may enjoy their felicities well out of my sight and earshot.

I have at home a dog, a charming animal.

We have the same tastes.

We prefer the country to the city.

When we sally forth for a walk, we insist on going by way of the hedge, the gutter, the pasture, and the bit of pine-wood.

We do not like cats, but we are a little jealous of them.

We like to lie on the rug and look at the fire.

And we prefer our meat a little underdone.

I have much more in common with my dog than I have with my neighbour.

Who is a celibate.

A Christian Scientist.

A vegetarian.

And plays talking records on the Victrola.

I received today a letter from a young woman who went to boarding-school with me. At least, she says she went to boarding-school with me. I do not remember her.

And on the strength of her having been to boarding-school with me, she wishes me to come and take tea with her, and talk over the old times.

Whose old times, hers or mine? Our past is not in common.

If she should talk over her old times, I should very likely fall asleep.

Should I talk over mine, she would undoubtedly leave the room.

I had an enemy.

He was a very good enemy.

I felt that I could rely on his hostility as on few things in this shifting life.

He was invariably inimical to my ideals, my aspirations, my opinions, even my welfare.

He publicly disparaged my work, my mental capacities, my moral stamina, my habits, and my figure.

In short, he hated my vitals.

Today, as I stood on my balcony, looking out over the Seine, I saw the postman cross the street and disappear in the doorway beneath me. A moment later there came a knock at my door, and the maid entered with an urgent note.

'After all—we are both Americans in a strange city—why not let bygones be bygones?'—will I take luncheon with him on Tuesday?

No, I will not.

I will lunch alone on Tuesday, with an open book beside my place.

In the first place, the fact that we both are Americans has nothing to do with it.

Had I wished to spend my life lunching with Americans, I need not have come to Paris.

In the second place, Paris is not a strange city.

If he feels it to be so, he might much better go back to Wichita at once.

In the third place, if I let bygones be bygones he is no longer my enemy.

And the fact that he is no longer my enemy not constituting him my friend, he becomes thus automatically a stranger to me.

And a stranger who has written me a presumptuous note.

Besides, I shall not be here on Tuesday.

It is now four o'clock in the afternoon.

At seven thirty-two, dear reader, I board the Orient Express for Constantinople.

But don't think for a moment I am going to Constantinople. Ah, no.

The most awful experience of my life was in Constantinople.

Four girlhood friends, their husbands, their babies, their nurse-maids, and their incessant and insufferable conversation, all, all at the same hotel as myself.

And me flat on my back with a broken ankle, as helpless as a cat in paper shoes.

Ah, no.

Somewhere between Paris and Constantinople, in the dead of night, in the silence of an uninhabited and uninhabitable land, at some lone and uncharted pumping-station, I shall lower myself softly forth from the window of my wagon-lit, and prayerfully watch the tail-lights winking on into the darkness.

And it will be days and days—

Possibly a week—

Before the virgin niece of the canned-corn king

Who married my father's dipsomaniac cousin's epileptic widow

Gaily pats the poison ivy curtaining the door of my cave and cries,

'Oh, here you are at last! I've had the awfulest time finding you! Do be a dear and come out with me while I buy some dress-shields!'

January Hath XXXI Days (Planetary Aspects, Remarkable Days, Etc.)

1. NEW YEAR'S DAY, 1925. Cabarets closed, New York City; dancing abolished. Many private houses raided. Sale of crêpe paper and coloured balloons prohibited. Two men surprised in Central Park with pockets full of confetti; and given sixty days each. Slogan HAPPY NEW YEAR changed by Act of Congress to VIRTUOUS NEW YEAR. Thousands of post-cards held up in the mails.

Cigarettes banned, 1926.

Mars in the house of Venus. Saturn in the House of Representatives. Mercury in the descendant. The hand of beneficent reform will make itself felt in this country. Avoid females. Ask favors of elderly people.

Anti-Tobacco Bill passed, 1926. Tremendous rise in prices of cabbages, dried leaves, horse-hair, corn-silk and pond-lily stems.

Partial eclipse of the sun. Mercury still going down.

7. OLD CHRISTMAS DAY. Santa Claus excommunicated by Society for Suppression of Imagination in Children, 1932. Any allusion, either public or private, to this fictitious and misleading character prohibited under heavy penalty.

All volumes of the untruthful adventures of (a) Alice in Wonderland, (b) Jack and the Beanstalk, (c) Little Red Riding-Hood, and (d) Cinderella, together with (e) the questionable episode of the Babes in the Wood; as well as the highly improbable tales of Hans Christian Andersen, and the senseless rhymes of Mary Vergoose: banned by S. S. I. C., removed from Public Libraries, and burned by Public

Executioner in Central Park, 1933. Whipping-posts set up on Riverside Drive; stocks in Wall Street.

Croquet, tiddledy-winks, and kindred games of chance abolished, 1934.

Mercury invisible. Saturn in the house of Mirth. An unfortunate day.

April Hath XXX Days

1. ALL FOOL'S DAY. Anthony Comstock[1] canonized, 1925. Proclaimed patron saint of America, 1926.

Famous speech of Senator Lovejoy to Congress, 1927: 'Ladies and gentlemen: though a woman speak with the tongues of men and of senators, and have not modesty, she has become as sounding zimbarimbaphones and tinkling tomato-cans! How many a meek and retiring woman, a contented and home-loving wife, the proud mother of fourteen bouncing little darlings, seldom setting foot outside her own cheerful and immaculate kitchen, once having lost her modesty, has not developed into a Cleopatra, a Sappho, a Helen of Troy! Beware, ladies, beware lest such a fate await one of you! Ladies and gentlemen, I have given my life, the lives of my wife and children, the sweat of my neighbour's brow, and over three of my father's hard-earned millions, in the holy cause of Female Modesty! A law requiring women to wear high-necked evening-gowns and ankle-length bathing-suits must be incorporated into the Constitution of this country, or civilization is at an end! It has repeatedly been brought to my attention that thousands of people, people in my very dooryard, so to speak, for lack of the funds necessary for further

---

1 Anthony Comstock (1844–1915), founder of the New York Society for the Suppression of Vice. His name became a byword for oppressive censorship, or 'Comstockery'.

research, are dying in agony every year of cancer!… But, ladies, and gentlemen, true to my principle, I have invariably replied, "What's a little cancer in comparison to loss of modesty?'"

Festival of St. Anthony, 1929. Four thousand men and women storm Metropolitan Museum, destroying most of the paintings and all the statuary.

Sale and consumption of tea and coffee prohibited, 1930.

William Jennings Bryan[2] proclaimed emperor, 1943.

The position of Billy Sunday[3] in the house of Jupiter points to much agitation among the heavenly bodies, and forbodes evil for theatres and places of amusement. The death of many prominent people is indicated, even Royalty may not escape.

7. OLD-LADY DAY. Music abolished, as being exciting to the lower instincts, 1935. Metropolitan Opera House and Carnegie Hall given over as picnicing-grounds to the Vicars' Anti-Art League and the Society for the Restoration of Side-Saddles for Women.

Ducking-stool for scolds installed on Boston Common, 1938.

Bill passed forbidding women to cut their hair even in case of fever, 1939.

Circulation of *The Tail of a Comet,* by Harold Bell Wright, suppressed, 1940. Subsequently brought out under the title, *The Caudal Appendage of a Comet.* All books by Gene Stratton-Porter banned and removed from Pubic Libraries, as laying unnecessary stress on the lamentable processes of reproduction among plants and animals, 1941.

---

2   William Jennings Bryan (1860–1925), a presidential nominee for the Democratic Party and later the Populist Party. He was a religious conservative who campaigned for schools to be banned from teaching Darwin's theory of evolution.

3   Billy Sunday (1862–1935), major-league baseball player who became a famous evangelical Christian preacher and advocate for the temperance movement.

Venus invisible. Carrie Nation[4] in Casiopoeia's Chair. Do not court, marry, or ask favors.

11. LOW SUNDAY. 25th Amendment, enforcing compulsory attendance at divine service on a minimum of fifty-two Sundays per annum, for a period of not less than eleven nor more than twenty-four hours per diem, adopted by Congress, 1943.

Philadelphia leads country in re-establishing Curfew, 1946. Any person or persons discovered abroad after the ringing of the Liberty Bell at 8:00 P. M., will be apprehended and confined in the pillory in Independence Square, during the period of the Emperor's pleasure.

Mercury invisible. Uranus refuses to rise before sunset. A very doubtful day.

July Hath XXXI Days

4. INDEPENDENCE DAY, 1776. Last Bacardi cocktail served in Brevoort grill, 1919. Unprecedented soaring in prices of soothing-syrup, lemon-extract, denatured alcohol, Sloane's Liniment and shoe-polish.

Over seven thousand illicit stills seized and confiscated, 1920.

Flag at half-mast on Internal Revenue Building, 1923.

Population of New York City, 23,000; 1925 census.

The conjunction of Neptune and Aquarius in the house of Bacchus has a threatening aspect as regards grain-crops, and the total eclipse of the Moon points to affliction in the Customs House. The Luminaries being just below the horizon in Square to Saturn

---

4   Carrie Nation (1846–1911), a radical temperance campaigner, notorious for attacking barrooms with a hatchet and smashing bottles, sometimes whilst praying.

threaten an early frost. Sell before noon, travel and remove.

13. Card-playing abolished, 1925.

Theatres closed, 1941.

Co-educational schools for all ages abolished, 1943.

Literature abolished, and all appurtenances thereto, including printing-presses, book-binderies, and pen-, ink-, and paper-plants confiscated by government and destroyed. Any person caught writing, reading, selling, buying, lending or borrowing A Book, liable to three years' penal servitude.

Motion before the House to do away with Summer, as being heating to the blood and inciting to venery, 1949.

Carried, 1950.

The unfortunate aspect of Apollo in the eclipse of Times Square, promises a dull season. The child born on this day will be steady and persevering and lead an uneventful life.

September Hath XXX Days

1. LABOR DAY. Twenty-eighth Amendment, requiring that every woman shall marry at or previous to the age of eighteen, and give birth to no less than sixteen children, two of which shall be more or less crippled, and one of which either (a) deaf-mute, (b) epileptic, or (c) imbecile, adopted by Congress, 1950.

All motion-picture houses closed and paraphernalia taken over by the Society for the Suppression of Youth among the Young, 1948.

Baseball goes, 1952.

Gemini in the ascendant. Total eclipse of the Sun. Avoid females.

6. A little band of smug and stiff-necked Puritans, including Miles Standish, John Alden, Priscilla Mullens, John Carver and William Brewster, spurning the indulgent arms of the generous, tolerant, broad-minded and sympathetic King James I, sailed from Plymouth, England, on the good

ship *Mayflower*, bound for the New World,—their slogan: FREEDOM TO WORSHIP GOD! (1620). A little band of nervous and repressed, but liberty-loving, men and women, including John Standish, Priscilla Carver, William Alden, Mary Mullens, and John Brewster, fleeing from the tyranny and despotism of the only absolute monarchy on the face of the globe, sail from Pymouth, New England, in the good ship *Cornflower* bound for the Old World,—their slogan: FREEDOM TO WORSHIP MAMMON! (1952).

(Note: Paris Observatory, Dec. 31, 1953. Total eclipse of the Western Hemisphere.)

ART AND HOW TO FAKE IT
Advice to the Art-Lorn

Dear Miss Boyd: Will you please tell me what is the matter with my studio? I am not an artist, but I am very artistic, and I have left no stone unturned to make my studio the very haunt of all that is free, etc., in the Village. I have a black floor, orange curtains, a ukulele made of a cigar-box, a leaky gas-jet, a back-number of a Russian newspaper, and as many cock-roaches, Chinese back-scratchers, and different shades of paint as anybody. Also I make a point of encouraging the milder vices, such as smoking; I have ash-trays everywhere. It has been the dream of my life to be a literary and artistic center, but somehow people do not flock as I had hoped they would do. If you can tell me what is the matter I shall be most grateful. Signed.

ARTISTIC.

(The trouble is with the ash-trays; remove them. Get into the habit when alone of crushing out your cigarette against the wall-paper, or dropping it in on the floor and carelessly grinding it into the rug, or tossing it in the general direction of the fire-place, if you have one, being very sure never to look anxiously after it to see where it lands. This easy manner on your part will do more than anything else to put your guests at ease. Soon they will be using your studio as if it were their own, going to sleep with their feet in the coffee-tray, wiping paint from their hair and elbows upon the sofa-pillows, making sketches on the walls of unclothed people with small heads and over-developed muscles, and dropping ashes just everywhere.)

Dear Miss Boyd: I have just decided to open a restaurant, and I have rented an old stable on Sullivan Street just south of the Square, which I think ought to make a terribly attractive restaurant. I don't know anything about cooking, but I think I can get somebody to do the cooking. I am writing to ask you three questions: How shall I furnish it? What shall I name it? What should be my attitude towards my clients? Very truly yours,

AMBITIOUS.

P.S. I had thought of naming it either *The Topaz Armadillo, The UltraViolet Brontosaurus*, or *The Boeotian Swine*. None of these has been used yet, so far as I know. But I shall do nothing until I hear from you. A.

(I would advise you against using any of the three names you mention. It is impossible to be sure that somebody else has not already taken them. If I were you I would call it simply The Stable, which is so obvious a name for a Greenwich Village restaurant that I am sure nobody has ever thought of it. As regards the furnishing and decoration, I would suggest that you make very few changes. Keep the stalls just as they are; in each of them put a table made of a wide plank supported by two saw-horses; let the seats be chopping-blocks, in one of which might be sticking jauntily a bright sharp axe. The walls should be enlivened with pieces of old harness,—bridles, blinders, bits, etc.,—as well as photographs of Black Beauty and the One-Horse Shay; and there must of course be a rusty horseshoe over the door. Let the restaurant be lighted with smoky kerosene lanterns, and barn-dance music be furnished by an old-style gramophone with a painted horn. Serve the food in charming, hand-painted, little mangers, or in little canvas bags embroidered in assorted wools, which fit neatly over the heads of the guests. Each guest should be supplied with a cunning little whip to crack if the fodder is slow in arriving. As for the food itself, I would suggest that here you diverge a bit from your general scheme, and serve, instead of dry oats and bran, half-cooked spaghetti, sticky Armenian pastries, and liqueur-glasses of sweetened Turkish mud. As for yourself, you should circulate among your guests freely, dressed in a gunny-sack adorned with coarse tassels of red rope. Assume the habit, too, of singling out each evening from among your clients some entire stranger, seating yourself beside him, hanging your arm about his neck, and daintily gobbling up the choice bits of his food; in this way you will not only acquire a reputation as a wit, but you will also keep sufficiently well-nourished.

N.B. Be sure you have a hay-loft, where the guests may recline after dinner. This is important. The loft should have no more pitch-forks in it than observance of the tradition requires, and should be lighted only by a tin of white beans.)

Miss N. Boyd,
Dear Madam:
I am a plain, honest woman, with a house in Waverly Place where I let Furnished Rooms to Artists. I have a lot of trouble with them. In the first place they are awfully careless about their Rooms, they never hang-up anything, there are always dirty shirts on the floor, to say nothing of bread-crusts and rinds of ham-bologna. I have an awful time with them. Then another thing when they are not laying abed all day so I cant get in to do up the work, they are trying to set the chimny on fire burning up oily rags and pieces of canvas all covered with paint, and setting up all night talk-talk-talking so as honest people cant get a wink of sleep. But all that, though theres no getting round it that its terrible trying and all that, is not the reason why I take my pen in hand to write you. Its about the rent. They don't pay it. I let it go and let it go and when finaly I do get up curage to say something about it, because

I suppose I have my rights just the same as Artists, all the time I am talking they draw pictures of me on the back of an envelope. Then they say, O, come on Ma, I thought you was a Patrun of the Arts. Whatever that may be. Then they promise to pay me the next day, because somebody is going to buy a picture off them, but next day comes and they ether say the same thing all over or else they're gone. Id hold their baggage, only they never have any, only an empty gin-bottle all daubed over with red and purple and undressed women, or a fancy-dress costume so holy and dirty its of no use to anybody or two or three copies of a magerzine called the little reveiw. What will I do, dear Miss Boyd, I thought seeing you knew so much about Artists mabe you might be able to tell me. With grateful appreciation in advance I remain, yours very truly,

LANDLADY.

(There's only one thing to do. You can't go through their clothes while they're asleep, because they always sleep in their clothes. And it's never any good serving a summons on them to appear in court; because they just don't appear. The only thing to do it this. Buy a tin bank and place it on the table in the hall. Above it tack the following placard:

FREE THINKERS! FREE LOVERS!
and FREE BOOTERS!

If you have any Heathen Pity in your Hearts Drop a Nickel
in the Slot for the Starving Baby-Anarchists of Russia!

WHO DOES NOT CONTRIBUTE TO THE CAUSE
OF ANARCHY IS MID-VICTORIAN!!!

I think you will have no further trouble.)

Dear Miss Boyd:

Mine is a strange case. I have always thought I should like to be an artist. Not because I care anything about art, for I don't, but because artists lead such a free life. As a little boy, I was different from my young companions: I did not like to study; I objected to going to bed directly after supper; and I was often discovered pulling the wings off flies, or stealing sweets from my little sister. Later, my disinclination to apply myself to any profession, such as the ministry, the law, etc., surpassed only by my unfailing instinct for the salacious passages in the novels which I read, caused my parents to believe that I must be artistic. They have sent me to New York to study art. But as I have no particular talent in any direction, being more versatile than intensive, I fear, I am somewhat at a loss. I can neither write, paint, model, sing, dance, play a musical instrument, design costumes, nor act, nor am I a sympathetic listener. What shall I do? Signed,

JURGEN.

(Remember this. When all else fails, two courses remain open to a man: he can always give lectures on the drama, or edit anthologies of verse; for neither of these is either talent or training necessary.)

Dear Miss Boyd: Will you kindly advise me how to furnish and decorate my new studio in 12th Street? I am not an artist, but I do not get on very well with my husband, so I thought I would get me a studio in 12th Street. Although I have no artistic capabilities, and am totally colour-blind, I can make extremely good coffee, so I am sure there will always be artists dropping in, and I want the place to be perfect in every detail. Also kindly suggest what subjects that artists will be likely to discuss, so that I can read up a little. Very sincerely,

A WIFE AND MOTHER.

(The safest thing is a Chinese studio; everybody has one, so nobody can criticize yours. The correct way to decorate it is as follows: Floor, black; ceiling, blue; walls, lemon-yellow, olive-green, cherry-red, plum-violet, respectively; curtains, persimmon-orange, made of tarlatan, unhemmed; couch on floor; cushions on floor, books on floor, tea-tray on floor, cigarette-butts on floor, guests on floor. Get everything you can find that is made of teak-wood,—you can always tell it: dull-black, lot of carving and mother-of-pearl. Everything that isn't teak-wood, paint vermilion. Have something lacquered; doesn't matter what. Have a lot of pictures of tom-cats and tigers around, also Japanese prints as follows: Little men going up hill in rain-storm; small tree with large bird in it; lady writing letter with paint-brush; lady shooting at shoji with bow and arrow; actor with tongue out of mouth. These are all very inexpensive; if you buy a tea-set in Mott Street, they will probably come wrapped around the cups. Be sure to burn incense night and day, with the windows closed; this cannot fail to give atmosphere.

As for conversation, the artists will talk about El Greco, Cézanne and Gauguin. It is safe to remark of El Greco, 'Well, look at Cézanne!'; of Cézanne, 'Still, look at Gauguin!'; and of Gauguin, 'Have you ever been to Tahiti?' You say you are colour-blind. Divulge the fact to no-one. But never lose the opportunity of describing in detail the colour-scheme of any landscape, smock, or picture at which you and your companions might be gazing. Your success is assured.)

Dear Miss Boyd: Since you have so much influence with the up-town thrill-hunters, can't you sort of give 'em a hint that the Village isn't fashionable any more? They're thicker down here than garbage-cans, little theatres, and Italian babies; they've bought up all the north-light, and hung batik over it; and the poor homeless native has not where to lay his chrome yellow and Prussian blue. Yours,

MATTISSE PICCASSO.

(The condition of which you complain will not continue long. Since the prohibition of spirituous liquors in the States, there has been an ever-increasing migration of the art-just-lovers from Harlem to Montparnasse. The *Quartier Latin* [Scandinavian Quarter] of Paris, is full of them.)

Dear Miss Boyd: I am Chinese girl, but attend American college, Vassar, and enjoy very much. My room-mate is very nice girl, blue eye, yellow hair, very pretty, but in one fact very peculiar. She insist on decorating room with old awful Chinese screen and picture and little ugly dog and Buddha which is not true god, also old piece of weaving made long time ago all by hand and most uneven by dirty peasant, all thing such as in my country no nice family permit be found in attic. In vain I exhort, O cherished room-mate, behold beautiful American golden-oak rocking-chair, behold wonderful miraculous American Victrola, behold incomparable American imitation lace, all, all made by machinery and without flaw!—In vain, in vain. She tack up on wall unspeakable object such as my baby-brother could do better, she offend my artistic eye with hideous Chinese teak-wood, table-atrocity, she break up our friendship. Advise me, most honourable Boyd. I am in despairs. Signed,

CHU CHIN CHOW.

(Unfortunately, this letter arrives too late for me to answer it.—N.B.)

I am so sick of things being put where I can't reach them, just to get them out of reach of the baby!

Of course, I was just as sorry as anybody when the baby swallowed the buttonhook and nearly died. But just the same, it's a disgusting spectacle,—a large family of grown men and women all going about with their shoes unbuttoned; and it does seem as though there might be a compromise.

It was father's idea. Father is crazy about the baby. Really, you'd think that weakness and helplessness were virtues, the admiration father has for them. One day after dinner he arose, placed one hand on the back of his chair and the other inside his weskit, and announced: that from that time on, whatsoever there might be in the house which could, under the most fantastic circumstances, endanger the health of a baby should be, by the aid of a derrick, hoisted to the high shelf in the storeroom, out of reach of us all.

Now when you consider how determined a baby always is to kill itself, and how little it really takes to kill a baby, and when you consider that 'the house', as father hastened to explain when he saw us all moving to the garage, comprises also the garage, the wash-house, the cook-house, the boat-house, the dog-kennel, the chapel and the ash-can,—you can readily imagine how full a life we lead since the day the baby ate the buttonhook.

It's an enormous house, ours. Some people don't care much for the style of architecture, because it wasn't built by the Egyptians, or the Romans, or the women of Tahiti; we built it ourselves, and nobody has quite forgiven us. But there's no denying that it's enormous; it has forty-five rooms (or forty-eight; I can never remember which). It has north, east, south and west exposure; and while it must be admitted that the north windows open on a court and the south on a back-yard, the fact that all the apartments in the east wing, as well as all those in the west wing, look out upon a very handsome ocean, rather more than makes up for it. Also, the plumbing is wonderful.

People used to love to come and visit us, because father is fairly well-to-do, and always gave everybody a wonderful time. There was always a queen or two dropping in to tea, and a grand duke to make a fourth at auction.

But since the day that all the rum—the only thing that made our tea bearable—and all the playing-cards, were put on the high shelf out of reach of the baby, there's been a decided lapse in our calling-list.

In the first place, we never invite anybody any more. At least, we children don't. We're ashamed to. Nothing to do but walk about on tip-toe and count the rooms, and the whole place smelling to heaven of odorless talc!

Except for the milk-man, who still calls regularly, nobody ever comes near the house at all. That is, of course there are still father's friends. But I mean, nobody interesting.

And people are beginning to snicker at the very mention of our name.

'Fyodor,' said my father to me one day, when he met me in the act of carrying a step-ladder into the store-room, 'a house divided against itself cannot stand.'

'I should worry,' I replied. 'Let it fall. It's time we had a new house.'

Whereat father flew into the most dreadful pet, and shut me in the closet without my luncheon. And that was that.

Father is a politician. He has spent the best years of his life in an endeavour to make the world safe for stupidity. It has been an up-hill struggle, but at last things begin to look as if his dream were about to come true.

Mother is more artistic. She is so artistic that if you strike *d* and *c* together on the piano, it sets her teeth on edge.

Of course, it's not as if we didn't try to reach the high shelf. You'd be astonished to see all the different kinds of step-ladders there *are* hidden about in those forty-eight rooms, all painted blue and red, or black and yellow, to make them look like rocking-horses. But it's terribly difficult. Because, though sometimes you manage to get high enough to pull something down, you never get high enough to see what it is you're pulling; you just take the first thing you touch, and pretend you're satisfied.

It's not as if it were a nice baby, jolly, sweet-tempered, bright, and all that. It's a nasty, sniveling baby. It has weak eyes and a weak tummy, there is always a pin sticking into somewhere, and it would rather howl than not.

And then, it's such a stupid baby. It's quite old, for a baby, but it can't walk a step. It won't try to walk, it's so afraid of a little tumble. So it crawls. But it crawls just everywhere.

And it can't talk, either. Of course, if you say to it, 'mama', 'horsie', 'capitalist', 'communism', 'art', it repeats the words after you; but it hasn't the faintest notion what it's saying.

I said to mother, once, that the baby was stupid. She did not deny it. But she said, 'All the more reason, then, that we should give up our lives for the little, helpless thing.'

'I don't see why,' I disagreed. 'It will always be stupid, no matter what we do.'

'Ah, yes,' signed my mother, piously rolling up her eyes toward the floor above, 'but the highest duty of the strong is to protect the weak. And to make them happy. What nobler life could a man wish, my son, than to pick up all day long the spoons which his neighbour throws upon the floor? We must not be proud. So long as he crawls, we must crawl, too. We must confine our conversation to words of one syllable or less. And, in order that he may never know his interiority, and have his feelings hurt, we must employ all our intelligence in an endeavour to make ourselves as stupid as he is.'

I was silent.

'What do you say!' pleaded my mother, gently and brightly, in the manner of one soliciting recruits in a holy cause.

'I say,' I retorted, turning on my heel and starting for the door, 'that it's a pity some-one doesn't drop a brick on his head.'

'For shame!' cried my parent, aghast. 'Your own little baby brother!'

There are quite a number of us in our family, and some of us really have talent. Fritz, the oldest boy, was always very musical. He was getting on very well, indeed he was well on the road to becoming a world-famous violinist. But since father put his fiddle on the top shelf out of reach of the baby, he has fallen off considerably in his technique. Of course, it *is* a handicap.

Isadora, the oldest girl, always wanted to be a dancer. But they wouldn't let her, because it would shake the house and wake the baby. She pleaded that there is a kind of dance where you don't lift your feet from the floor. But they said they didn't believe that was really dancing. And so they wouldn't let her, anyhow. (She became, finally, an instructor of calisthenics in a girls' school.)

Sara might have been a great actress. She had a marvelous voice. She never opened her mouth but a little chill went up and down your spine, and you wanted to laugh and cry and kiss her shoes. But of course, if people won't let you speak above a whisper—well, she's gone into the movies, now, and is making *piles* of money.

It was just the same with Enrico, only his was a singing voice. He died, not long ago, obscure, untended, and heart-broken. I couldn't help thinking how different it might have been, if only he'd been brought up in a different family.

As for me, Fyodor, I always wanted to be a novelist. And for years I have given up all my time to writing. Lately, of course, they have put my pen and ink and typewriter on the top shelf out of reach of the baby, which *is* a handicap. But in spite of that, with the aid of a burnt match, the only kind of match we are permitted to have in the house, I keep on. I have written books which, could you read them, would tear up your world from its foundations and build it again, would allay for all time the ills which now assail you, and provide you with others, books which would rend your soul, wring your heart, and stretch your mind to the point of physical pain. But you will never read them. For, as as fast as I write them, they are put on the top shelf out of baby's reach.

Of course most of us,—and there are a great many more, whom I have not mentioned—have left home. As for those of us who remain, it is not so much that we remain as that we haven't gone yet.

Only yesterday I had a post-card from Pablo, the last of us to leave. Pablo is a painter,—and it *was* difficult for him, having his palette and all his paints on the top shelf, out of reach of the baby. He has gone to a place where the top shelf is on a level with the wainscoting. 'Am having a fine time,' he writes. 'Wish you were here.' And do you know, I've half a mind to go.

Except for one circumstance, I should have been a great sculptor; or let us say, rather, to be exact, like the late M. Rodin a mighty modeler in clay.

And I would to heaven that on the twenty-first of March in the year of our dubious salvation nineteen hundred and twenty, I had remained quietly in my motel in the rue d'Antin, and cut my own hair.

What ever became of her, that blue-eyed woman in mink, who slipped into my palm one day the address of a beauty-parlor in the rue de Rivoli, and left me, smiling, I do not know. And it is as well for us both.

I was free, and my life was before me. And what I was to do with that life, I knew well. I cared but little for the society of men, still less for that of the members of my own sex; I was content to be alone. I was not harassed by a desire to become a great actress, or to amass a large fortune. The feel of the cold gray mud in my two hands was happiness enough.

As may be imagined, I gave but little thought to my personal appearance. The shape of my head was well enough, my neck was not short, my second toe was longer than the first. I bathed regularly, with plain soap and a stiff brush, cleaned my teeth twice a day, washed my hair before it needed it, and kept my nails filed to the ends of my fingers. I dressed simply, and fairly well. I came and went about my business exciting no comment.

The one office which I found it difficult to perform for myself was the cutting of my hair.

As long as I remained in England this did not greatly matter. I had a friend, an excellent person, whose delight it was sternly to shear me and fiercely to clip me up the back.

But it so happened that early in the year 1920 my fortunes called me to take up my residence on the Continent. I came to Paris. And on the twenty-first of March of that year I was moved to enter a hair-dressing establishment hard by the equestrienne statue of Jeanne d'Arc in the rue de Rivoli.

All that I wanted was a hair-cut, a simple manipulation of scissors about my ears. That was all I wanted, and I said as much. It should have cost me three francs.

A black-eyed man with a small waist and smelling of violets appeared before me, wringing his hands. He placed a chair at my back and bowed me into it. Deftly but not without tenderness he wrapped me in a large white apron and tucked a towel into my collar.

'Friction?' said he.

'No,' said I, 'hair-cut.'

'Shampoo?' said he, 'singe? a little *coup de fer?*'

'No,' said I, 'hair-cut. Just plain hair-cut.'

He seized a comb, raked my hair violently back from my forehead, parted it in two places, pinched it, and rubbed it between his fingers.

'Ah,' said he, 'Madam has their hair beautiful *comme tout*, mais le scalp very dry. She is *habituée* to employ an anticalvitique, no?'

'No,' I replied, 'whatever that may be. I am not habituated to employ anything. Kindly cut my hair at once or hand me the scissors. I am in a hurry.'

He sighed windily, and clasped his hands beneath his chin. '*Madame a tort!*' said he.

He reached for an atomizer, and as if I had been a half finished bust, sprayed me, with scented water.

After which he cut my hair, not badly, clipped my neck, blew the chaff from my neck with a large hot breath, powdered me, brushed me, and thrust a mirror into my hand, at the same time addressing me rapidly in French.

'Very good,' I replied, considering my reflection in the mirror.

Whereupon he caught me by the shoulder, drew me to a large basin of mottled red marble, depressed my head with a heavy hand, and all but drowned me in a sudden flow of scalding suds.

I came up choking and spluttering.

'Are you crazy?' I cried.

He laughed loud and long, and pushed me merrily back into the basin.

I sought to expostulate, but my mouth was full of soap and my ears ringing.

'Camomile?' he cried.

'No!' I shrieked with my expiring breath.

But he did not hear me.

'The serviette will protect the eyes,' he said, placing in my grasp a towel, which I clutched with gratitude, and applied to my smarting vision.

He scratched me, rinsed me, wrung me, and drew me backward by the hair to the chair in which I had originally been seated. He wound a cloth about my head and pressed upon it heavily. Then, pushing a plug into the wall, he brought up beside me a great steel mouth with a twisted woven tail.

A hurricane hotter than the dry breath of the Sahara, roaring like a lion and smelling foully of gas, lifted my hair and whipped it before me.

I heard a voice from very far away.

'Friction?' it seemed to have said.

It did not occur to me to reply.

I saw a fat bottle disappear abruptly from its niche on the shelf. Simultaneously a wave of perfume broke over me.

'Manicure?' came the voice again, curiously caressing.

I clenched my fists and hid my nails desperately in the

palms of my hands.

My hand was forced open, and the nails regarded coldly.

'Manicure!' shouted the voice.

Instantly a large presence in black silk and smelling of carnations was in the room. A small table was set up beside me, and my elbow sunk in damp soft cushion.

The presence in black attacked me forthwith and without mercy.

Rhythmically, as she filed one finger, the end of the file stung like a wasp the next finger. The pain was intense, but it did not occur to me to protest.

When she had finished with one hand, she thrust it into a bowl of boiling soap, and grasped the other. She thrust back the cuticle cruelly, with a hard instrument; she lacerated it with scissors.

She applied white paste and red. She polished my nails until the ends of my fingers smoked.

'Madame has been here a long time?' said the woman by way of conversation.

'Years,' I whispered, putting my hand to my brow. I thought of my peaceful home in the little vegetarian town of Letchworth, Hertz., and tears suffused my eyes.

'Massage?' said the woman, brightly.

I blinked at her through my tears.

'Massage?' she repeated, in a happy tone.

'You know best,' I sighed.

She squeezed my hands ardently, poured over them a milky fluid from a bottle marked *Lait du Citron*, dried them in her apron, patted them, and prepared to rise. The wind in my hair, which all this time had been wailing and howling like the soul of a poet in Purgatory, sobbed now and died away. After a whispered conversation at my back, I was seized and borne off to another part of the establishment.

I was deposited in another chair before another mirror. A towel was wound about my hair, and framed my gray face whitely. Bits of cotton were tightly wedged under this bandage at intervals. 'Madame is accustomed to have her face massaged regularly?'

'This is the first time,' I replied with shame.

'*Madame a tort,*' she sighed.

I closed my eyes.

A cream smelling of almonds was spanked upon my cheeks and rubbed into them. Cool water scented with roses was splashed into my face. A grease reeking of camphor was applied. I felt firm paths beneath my chin, soft fingers at the corners of my eyes. Hot needles, like a tiny but powerful shower-bath, pricked me all over.

I have no recollection of leaving this room and returning to the other.

It may be that I fell asleep. It may be that I fainted.

In any case, when I came to my senses, I was seated once more in the room which I had first entered.

The odor of violets was all about me. A comb was being drawn through my hair savagely. Over an intense gas flame high up on the wall two pairs of curling-tongs were glowing red.

I arose with a shriek and seized the hand of my tormentor.

'*Ça fait mal?—Pardon,*' he apologised delicately.

'You are not going to curl my hair,' I cried. 'I won't have it! My hair curls naturally, and I won't have it touched!'

He smiled benignly. 'One little *coup* to turn under the ends, that is all.'

'I won't have it touched!' I shouted.

'*Madame a tort,*' he replied with calmness, and reached for the irons.

I was helpless in his hands. I dared not move, for fear I should be branded. I sat fearfully still, and let him have his way.

Smoke arose from my head. A strong smell of burning hair filled the room. I sobbed aloud, but made no comment.

It would be useless as well as harrowing to prolong the story of that fatal afternoon. I escaped at length, fled from the shop barefoot, with a white apron flying from my shoulders and the large neck of a broken hammermelis bottle in my hand, leapt into a moving taxi, babbled the address of the American Express Company, and lost consciousness.

I awoke in my bed in my hotel in the rue d'Antin.

On opening my eyes, the first object I beheld was a gigantic brown-paper parcel on the table beside me.

I stared at it for some time without recognition or interest.

Finally I arose, not without difficulty, and limped across the room for my scissors. I cut the cords of the parcel and poured out its contents upon the bed.

Paste of Almonds, Milk of Lemons, Sugar of Peaches, Water of Roses, Lotion of Oranges, Cucumbers' Blood; scalp-tonics, skin-tonics, preparations to remove hair, preparations to promote its growth; bleaches, dyes, rouges, powders, perfumes, brilliantines, water-softeners, bath-salts; sponges, plasters, brushes, pads; eye-brighteners, wrinkle-eradicators, and freckle-removers.

And with these was the bill, paid for me at the desk while I slept, and added to my account at the hotel—eight hundred and sixty francs and twenty-five centimes.

I arose in a despair too deep for tears, and removed the articles from the bed. I ranged them upon the bureau, the dresser, the shelf in the bath-room, the writing-desk, and the top of my wardrobe-trunk. The wrappers which I removed filled the waste-basket and overflowed upon the floor.

A warm and varied odor arose from the basket. I dropped to my knees beside it and buried my face in the scented paper.

As I lifted my eyes, I caught for the first time, in the mirror of the *armoire à glace,* my reflection.

I stared, unbelieving.

I arose, trembling, seated myself before my dressing-table, and gazed for a long time into the glass.

No, there was no mistake. I was beautiful. My skin was smoother and whiter than an infant's; my cheeks were a delicate rose, my lips were carmine. My brows were a thin dark line; my lashes cast shadows on my cheek. My hair was a mass of gentle undulations, and its colour—its colour was the most wonderful thing I had ever seen.

From that day to this I am slave to the most exacting of tyrants.

Three times a week I pass through a certain portal in the rue de Rivoli, and deliver myself up into the hands of my creators. Daily, night and morning, long weary hours, while the world sleeps, while the world canters in the Bois de Boulogne, I sit before my mirror, patting, steaming, brushing. I will not grow old. I will be beautiful always.

It was at one time my great delight to travel. I thought I should live to see all quarters of the globe. But more troublesome than plaster casts to pack and transport from place to place, are the thousand jars and bottles of a woman's beauty. I could not sleep at night in my *wagon-lit*, for thinking of my trunks behind in the luggage-van. What would I find this time at the end of the journey? What unguent spilled, what hats and gowns destroyed? For I clothe myself now in the perishable fabrics of the *chic*.

Wrinkles came, from worry, and my hair turned white.

I saw to that.

But it was cheaper, in the long run, quietly to settle down in Paris.

There comes over me at times a longing for the old free days, a desire to hold damp clay in my hands once more. But one glance at my nails, so rosy, so roundly pointed, so softly bright, so exquisite from the loving care of years—and I know that I shall never work again.

All that is in the past. Let it be.

The future holds its own bitter struggle.

INDEX OF TITLES